The Pilgrimage Series

THE DICKENS COUNTRY

CHARLES DICKENS IN 1857.

From a hitherto unpublished photograph by Mason.

THE DICKENS COUNTRY

BY

FREDERIC G. KITTON

AUTHOR OF

"CHARLES DICKENS BY PEN AND PENCIL," "DICKENS AND HIS ILLUSTRATORS,"
"CHARLES DICKENS: HIS LIFE, WRITINGS, AND PERSONALITY,"
"DICKENSIANA," ETC.

WITH

FORTY-EIGHT FULL-PAGE ILLUSTRATIONS
MOSTLY FROM PHOTOGRAPHS
BY T. W. TYRRELL

LONDON
ADAM AND CHARLES BLACK
1911

First published February, 1905
Reprinted September, 1911

INTRODUCTION

IT seems but a week or two ago that Frederic Kitton first mentioned to me the preparation of the volume to which I have now the melancholy privilege of prefixing a few words of introduction and valediction. It was in my office in Covent Garden, where he used often to drop in of an afternoon and talk, for a spare half-hour at the end of the day, of Dickens and Dickensian interests. We were speaking of a book which had just been published, somewhat similar in scope to the volume now in the reader's hand, and Kitton, with that thoroughly genial sympathy which always marked his references to other men's work, praised warmly and heartily the good qualities which he had found in its composition. Then, quite quietly, and as though he were alluding to some entirely unimportant side-issue, he added: "I have a book rather on the same lines on the stocks myself, but I don't know when it will get finished." That was a little more than a year ago, and in the interval how much has happened! The book has, indeed, "got finished" in the pressure of that indefatigable industry which his friends knew so well, but its author was never to see it in type. Almost before it had received his finishing touches, the bright, kindly, humane spirit of Frederic Kitton was "at rest and forever." He died on Saturday, September 10, 1904, and left the world appreciably poorer by the loss of a sincere and zealous student, a true and generous man.

As I turned over the pages of the book in proof, and recalled this passing conversation, it seemed to me that the whole character of its author was displayed, as under a sudden light, in that quite unconscious attitude of his towards the two books—the one his friend's, the other his own. For no one that I ever met was freer from anything like literary jealousy or the spirit of rivalry in art; no one was ever more modest concerning his own achievements. And in this case, it must be remembered, he was speaking of a

v

particular piece of work for which no writer in England was so well qualified as himself. His work had its limitations, and he knew them well enough himself. For treatment of a subject on a broad plane, critically, he had little taste; indeed, many of his friends may remember that at times, when they may have indulged too liberally in a wide literary generalization, he was inclined, quietly and almost deprecatingly, to suggest some single contrary instance which seemed to throw the generalization out of gear at once. He saw life and literature like a mosaic; his eye was on the pieces, not upon the piece; and this microscopic view had its inevitable drawbacks and hindrances. On the other hand, when it came to a subject like that of the present volume, his method was not only a good one, but positively the best and only certain method possible. His laborious care for detail, his unfailing accuracy—never satisfied till he had traced the topic home under his own eye—his loving accumulation of little facts that contribute to the general impression—all these conspicuous traits made him the one man qualified to speak upon such a subject with confidence and authority. One sometimes felt that he knew everything there was to know about Dickens and the circle in which Dickens lived. The minuteness of his knowledge could only be appreciated by those who had occasion to test it in actual conversation, in that give-and-take of question and answer by which showy, shallow information and pretentious ignorance are so quickly discomfited and exposed. He had not only, for example, traced almost every published line and letter of Dickens himself, but he could tell you, in turning over old numbers of *Household Words*, the author of every single inconsiderable contribution to that journal; he was familiar with the manner and the production of all the *infusoria* of Wellington Street. It was a wonderful wealth of information, and his habit of acquiring and fostering it was born and bred in his very nature. In this, as in many other respects, he was essentially his father's son.

When I ventured, a page further back, to call his method "microscopic," the word slipped naturally from my pen, but in a moment its indisputable propriety asserted itself. Frederic George Kitton was trained in the school of microscopy. He was born at Norwich on May 5, 1856, and his father, who had then only just completed his twenty-ninth year, was already known among his associates as a scientist of much research and no little originality of observation. Frederic Kitton the elder was the son of a Cambridge ironmonger, and had been intended for the legal profession; but his father's business did not prosper, and the whole family was obliged to remove to Norwich, there to take up work in a wholesale tobacco business, the proprietor of which was one Robert Wigham, a botanist of some repute. This Mr. Wigham soon saw that Kitton was a clever lad, and, finding him interested in the studies which were his own diversion, trained him in botany and other scientific branches of research. The young man soon surpassed his tutor in knowledge and resource, and by the time that he was married and the father of our own friend, Frederic George Kitton, he had made a name among the leading diatomists of his time, and was reputed to be more successful in finding rare specimens than any other man in the country. His reputation and his industry increased together, with the result that the son grew up in an atmosphere of unsparing research and conscientious accuracy of observation which never failed him as an example for life. We may fairly attribute the general outlines of F. G. Kitton's method to the inspiration he received at his father's desk.

This inspiration found its first expression upon the lines of art. The boy showed great ability with his pencil, and was apprenticed to wood engraving, joining the staff of the *Graphic*, and contributing any number of pencil drawings and woodcuts to its columns, in the days before the cheap processes of reproduction had supplanted these genuine forms of art-workmanship. His landscapes and his pictures of old buildings and romantic architecture were full of breadth and feeling, and some of the best of them were devoted to an early book of travel in the Dickens country, in which he collaborated with the late Willam R. Hughes. Indeed, much of the most picturesque work of his life was done in the way of black and white.

At the age of twenty-six, however, he decided to be less of an artist and more of a writer, and retired finally from the ranks of illustrated journalism. He settled about this time at St. Albans in Hertfordshire, and began his long series of books, most of them dedicated to his lifelong study of Dickens and his contemporaries. His first books of the kind treated, not unnaturally, of the various illustrators of Dickens's novels, and monographs on Hablot K. Browne and John Leech attracted attention for their fidelity and sympathetic taste. Following these came " Dickensiana : a Bibliography of the Literature relating to Charles Dickens and His Writings" (1886); " Charles Dickens by Pen and Pencil" (1890);

"Artistic London : from the Abbey to the Tower with Dickens" (1891) ; "The Novels of Charles Dickens : a Bibliography and a Sketch" (1897) ; "Dickens and His Illustrators" (1899) ; "The Minor Writings of Charles Dickens" (1900) ; "Charles Dickens : His Life, Writings, and Personality" (1902) ; and innumerable editorial works, among which must be mentioned his notes to the Rochester Edition of Dickens, his recension of Dickens's verse, and his general conduct of the Autograph Edition now in course of publication in America—a laborious undertaking, which included a series of bibliographical notes from his pen of the very first value to all students of " Dickensiana." He had also in MS. a valuable dictionary of Dickens topography, illustrated by descriptive quotations from the novels themselves ; and, finally, he left the " copy " for the present book, which will rank among the most useful and characteristic of all his contributions to the study of the author whom he so much admired and so sincerely served.

Kitton was only forty-eight when he died, and the work which he had done was large in bulk and rich in testimony to his industry ; but he was far from accomplishing the volume of work which he had already set before himself. It is no secret that the short " Life of Dickens " which he published two and a half years ago was only regarded by himself as the framework upon which he proposed to construct a much more elaborate biography, to be at least as long as Forster's " Life," fortified by a vast array of facts which Forster had not been disposed, or careful enough, to collect. The book would have been full of material and value ; but there were some of us who believed that Kitton's talent might be even better employed in a work which none but himself could have satisfactorily accomplished—the preparation of an elaborate annotated edition of Forster, constructed upon the scale of Birkbeck Hill's monumental Boswell, and illustrated by all the fruits of Kitton's profitable research. We talked the matter over together, and he was enthusiastically willing to essay the task. But obstacles arose at the moment, and now the work can never be done as he would have done it. His talent was peculiarly adapted to annotation ; his knowledge of the subject was unparalleled. If the work is ever done (and I suppose it is bound to be done some day), it can never be done now with that surety and deliberate finality which he would have had at his disposal.

But one must not speak of Kitton only as a student of literature and an artist ; any picture of him that seemed to suggest that he was rooted to his desk and his desk-work, to the exclusion of outside interests and social activities, would give a very false impression of his energetic and amiable temperament. There are many books standing to Kitton's name in the catalogue of the British Museum, and innumerable articles of his writing in the files of the reviews, magazines, and newspapers of the last twenty years, but his work extended far beyond the limits of print and paper. He was not only an industrious man of letters, but a most helpful and self-sacrificing citizen. His adopted town of St. Albans, and the county of Hertfordshire at large, had no little cause for gratitude in all he did in their interests. Despite the amount of literary work he got through, there was scarcely a day that passed without finding him at work at the Hertfordshire County Museum, where he took sole charge of the prints and books, a collection which his care and judgment made both exhaustive and invaluable. He was continually at work, arranging and adding to the books and prints, and outside the walls of the museum he did inestimable service in preserving the ancient buildings of the town of St. Albans. Had it not been for his intervention, many of the most interesting old houses in the town would have been pulled down ; he argued with callous owners and vandal jerry-builders, and managed to retain for the town those characteristic and historic buildings around the abbey which in days to come will be the chief attraction of the picturesque county town he loved to serve.

And so, with hard work at his desk and unsparing energy out of doors, his bright, unselfish spirit wore itself out. He never looked strong, but I do not think he seemed actually ill when one spring morning in this last year he came in to see me at my office, and told me, with his easy, unapprehensive smile, that he was about to undergo an operation. "It is only a small matter," he said, "but the doctors say I ought to have it done. I hope I shall soon be back again, and we will have a further talk over that book you know about." We parted, as men part at the cross-roads, feeling sure of meeting on the morrow. But I never saw him again. The operation he had made so light of proved too much for a constitution already undermined by hard, unselfish work. He lingered on, but never really rallied, and the end came very quietly, to close a life that had always brought with it a sense of peace and gentle will, wherever it had touched, whomsoever it had influenced.

For, when other shifting recollections of Frederic Kitton fade away—accidents of a common interest, chances of a brief and busy acquaintanceship—the impression that remains, and will always remain with those who knew him, is the haunting impression of a sweet and winning simplicity, an absolute sincerity of life and word, that knew no use for the thing he said but that it should be the thing he thought, and that never (so it seemed) thought anything of man, or woman, or child but what was kind and Christian and noble-hearted. He looked you in the eyes in a fearless, open fashion, as a man who had nothing to conceal and nothing to pretend ; he smiled with a peculiarly sunny and unhesitating smile, as one who had tried life and found it good. And yet, as the common rewards of life go, he had less cause to be thankful than many who complain ; he had to work hard (how hard it is not ours to say) for the ordinary daily gifts of homely comfort. He had little time to rest or play, and little means of recreation. Yet no friend of his, I believe, however intimate, ever heard him grumble about work and the badness of the times. He had a happy home, bright and blithe with the carol of the cricket on the hearth, and brighter and blither for his own affectionate nature ; and his happy spirit seemed to ask for nothing that lay outside the four walls of his plain contentment. He knew the secret of life— a simple secret, but hard to find, and harder to remember. He had no touch of self in all his composition, no taint of self-interest or self-care. He lived for others : and in their memory he will survive so long as earthly recollections and earthly examples return to encourage and to inspire.

ARTHUR WAUGH.

PUBLISHERS' NOTE.

OWING to the untimely death of the author, the page proofs were not revised by him for the press, though Mr. Kitton corrected proofs at an earlier stage.

Mr. Kitton's friends—Mr. B. W. Matz, Mr. T. W. Tyrrell, and Mr. H. Snowden Ward—have kindly read the final proofs, without, however, making any material alterations.

CONTENTS

LIST OF ILLUSTRATIONS

From Photographs by T. W. Tyrrell, etc.

xiii

I MILE END TERRACE, PORTSEA
(NOW 393 COMMERCIAL ROAD, PORTSMOUTH). (*Page* 2.)

The birthplace of Charles Dickens.

THE DICKENS COUNTRY

CHAPTER I.

PORTSMOUTH AND CHATHAM.

THE writer of an article in a well-known magazine conceived the idea of preparing a map of England that should indicate, by means of a tint, those portions especially associated with Charles Dickens and his writings. This map makes manifest the fact that the country thus most intimately connected with the novelist is the south-eastern portion of England, having London as the centre and Rochester as the "literary capital," and including the counties of Norfolk, Suffolk, Essex, Kent, Surrey, Sussex, Hampshire, and Warwickshire, with an offshoot extending to the northern boundary of Yorkshire.

All literary pilgrims, and particularly the devotees of Charles Dickens, regard as foremost among literary shrines inviting special homage the scene of the nativity of "Immortal Boz." Like the birthplaces of many an eminent personage who first saw the light in the midst of a humble environment, the dwelling in which Dickens was born is unpretentious enough, and remains unaltered. The modest abode

3

rented shortly after marriage by John Dickens (the future novelist's father), from June, 1809, to June, 1812, stands in Commercial Road, Portsmouth, the number of the house having been recently changed from 387 to 393. The district was then known as Landport, in the Island of Portsea, but is now incorporated with Portsmouth ; a comparatively rural locality at that time, it has since developed into a densely populated neighbourhood, covered with houses and bisected by the main line of the municipal tramways.* It is, however, yet within the memory of middle-aged people when this area of brick and mortar consisted of pasture land in which trees flourished and afforded nesting-places for innumerable birds—a condition of things recalled by the names bestowed upon some of the streets hereabouts, such as Cherry Garden Lane and Elm Road—but now "only children flourish where once the daisies sprang."

The birthplace of Charles Dickens, which less than half a century ago overlooked green fields, is an interesting survival of those days of arboreal delights ; and the broad road, on the west side of which it is situated, leads to Cosham and the picturesque ruin of Porchester Castle. In 1809 John Dickens was transferred from Somerset House to the Navy Pay-Office at Portsmouth Dockyard, and, with his young wife, made his home here, in which

* Almost the whole of the Isle of Portsea, with the old parishes of Portsmouth and Portsea, is now included in the Borough of Portsmouth, Landport being one of the divisions of the ancient parish of Portsea ; while the old Portsmouth parish still remains but a small one, that of Portsea is of considerable dimensions, and divided into several parishes. One of the streets east of Commercial Road is called "Dickens Street," in honour of the novelist.

were born their first child (Frances Elizabeth) in 1810, and Charles on February 7, 1812. This domicile is a plain, red-brick building containing four rooms of moderate size and two attics, with domestic offices; in front there is a small garden, separated from the public roadway by an iron palisading; and a few steps, with a hand-rail, lead from the forecourt to the hooded doorway of the principal entrance. The front bedroom is believed to be the room in which Dickens was born. From the apartments in the rear there is still a pleasant prospect, overlooking a long garden, where flourishes an eminently fine specimen of the tree-mallow. On the death of Mrs. Sarah Pearce, the owner and occupier (and last surviving daughter of John Dickens's landlord), the house was offered for sale by public auction on Michaelmas Day, 1903, when, much to the delight of the townspeople as well as of all lovers of the great novelist, it was purchased by the Portsmouth Town Council for preservation as a Dickens memorial, and with the intention of adapting it for the purposes of a Dickens Museum. The purchase price was £1,125, a sum exceeding by five hundred pounds the amount realized on the same occasion by the adjoining freehold residence (No. 395), which is identical in character—an interesting and significant testimony as to the sentimental value attaching to the birthplace of "Boz."

Charles Dickens, like David Copperfield, was ushered into the world "on a Friday," and, when less than a month old, underwent the ordeal of baptism at the parish church of Portsea, locally and popularly known as St. Mary's, Kingston, and dating from the reign of Edward III. In 1882 a plan for its restoration and enlargement was proposed, but a few years later the authorities resolved to demolish it altogether and build a larger parochial church from designs by Sir Arthur Blomfield, A.R.A., the foundation stone of which was laid by Queen Victoria early in the spring of 1887, one half of the estimated cost being defrayed by an anonymous donor. On its completion the people of Portsmouth expressed a desire to perpetuate the memory of Charles Dickens by inserting in the new building a stained-glass window, but were debarred by a clause in the novelist's will, where he conjured his friends on no account to make him " the subject of any monument, memorial, or testimonial whatever," as he rested his claim to the remembrance of his country upon his published works. It is not common knowledge that three baptismal names were bestowed upon Dickens, viz., Charles John Huffam, the first being the Christian name of his maternal grandfather, the second that of his father, while the third was the surname of his godfather, Christopher Huffam (incorrectly spelt "Huffham" in the church register), who is described in the London Postal Directory of that time as a "rigger in His Majesty's Navy"; he lived at Limehouse Hole, near the lower reaches of the Thames, which afterwards played a conspicuous part in "Our Mutual Friend" ("Rogue Riderhood dwelt deep and dark in Limehouse Hole, amongst the riggers, and the mast, oar, and block-makers, and the boat-builders, and the sail-lofts, as in a kind of ship's hold stored full of waterside characters, some no better than himself, some very much better, and none much worse"). It is interesting to know that the actual font used at the ceremony of Charles Dickens's baptism has been preserved, and is now in St. Stephen's Church, Portsea.

John Dickens, after a four years' tenancy of No. 387, Mile End Terrace, went to reside in Hawke Street, Portsea. Here he remained from Midsummer Day, 1812, until Midsummer Day, 1814, when he was recalled to London by the officials at Somerset House.

I have spared no trouble in endeavouring to discover the house in Hawke Street which John Dickens and his family occupied. Mr. Robert Langton, in his " Childhood and Youth of Charles Dickens " (second edition), states that it is the " second house past the boundary of Portsea," which, however, is not very helpful, as the following note (kindly furnished by the Town Clerk of Portsmouth) testifies :

" I cannot understand what the connection can be between Hawke Street and the borough boundary. The town of Portsea, no doubt, had a recognised boundary, because at one time the greater part of it was encircled by ramparts, but Hawke Street did not come near those ramparts. The old borough boundary was outside the ramparts, both of Portsmouth and Portsea, and therefore Hawke Street did not touch that boundary. Since then the borough boundary has been extended on more than one occasion, and, of course, these boundaries could not touch Hawke Street." A letter sent by me to the Portsmouth newspapers having reference to this subject brought me into communication with a Southsea lady, who informs me that an old gentleman of her acquaintance (an octogenarian) lived in his youth at No. 8, Hawke Street, and he clearly remembers that the Dickens family resided at No. 16. Hawke Street, in those days, he says, was a most respectable locality, the tenants being people of a good class, while there were superior lodging-houses for naval officers who desired to be within easy reach of their ships in the royal dockyard, distant about five minutes' walk. No. 16, Hawke Street is a house of three floors and a basement ; three steps lead to the front door, and there are two bay-windows, one above the other. The tenant whom John Dickens succeeded was Chatterton, harpist to the late Queen Victoria.

Forster relates, as an illustration of Charles Dickens's wonderfully retentive memory, that late in life he could recall many minor incidents of his childhood, even the house at Portsea (*i.e.*, his birth-place in Commercial Road), and the nurse watching him (then not more than two years old) from " a low kitchen window almost level with the gravel walk " as he trotted about the " small front garden " with his sister Fanny.

Dickens's memory obviously failed him on this point, for he was a mere infant of barely five months old when his parents left Commercial Road to reside in Hawke Street, a fact which he had probably forgotten, and of which Forster had no knowledge, as no mention is made by him of the latter street. Here the family had lived two years when John Dickens was recalled to London. I therefore venture to suggest that the novelist vaguely recalled certain incidents of his childhood associated with Hawke Street. True, there is no " small front garden " at No. 16 (indeed, all the houses here are flush with the sidewalk), but at the back is a garden overlooked by the kitchen window, which has an old-fashioned, broad window-seat.

On quitting Portsea for the Metropolis, John Dickens and his family occupied lodgings in Norfolk Street (now Cleveland Street), on the east side of the Middlesex Hospital. In a short time, however, he was again "detached," having received instructions to join the staff at the Navy Pay-Office at Chatham Dockyard. The date of departure is given by Forster as 1816, and in all probability the Dickens family again took lodgings until a suitable home could be found. After careful research, the late Mr. Robert Langton discovered that from June, 1817 (probably midsummer), until Lady Day, 1821, their abode was at No. 2 (since altered to No. 11), Ordnance Terrace. There little Charles passed some of the happiest years of his childhood, and received the most durable of his early impressions.

Chatham, on the river Medway, derives its name from the Saxon word *Ceteham* or *Cættham*, meaning "village of cottages." It is anything but a "village" now, having since that remote age developed into a river port and a populous fortified town. Remains of Roman villas have been found in the neighbourhood, thus testifying to its antiquity. Chatham is one of the principal royal shipbuilding establishments in the kingdom. The dockyard was founded by Elizabeth before the threatened invasion of the Spanish Armada, and removed to its present site in 1662 ; it is now nearly two miles in length, and controlled by an Admiral-Superintendent, with a staff of artisans and labourers numbering about five thousand. Dickens describes and mentions Chatham in several of his writings, and in one

of the earliest he refers to it by the name of
" Mudfog."*

In "The Seven Poor Travellers" he says of
Chatham : "I call it this town because if anybody
present knows to a nicety where Rochester ends and
Chatham begins, it is more than I do."†

Mr. Pickwick's impressions of Chatham and the
neighbouring towns of Rochester, Strood, and
Brompton were that the principal productions
"appear to be soldiers, sailors, Jews, chalk, shrimps,
officers, and dockyard men," and that "the com-
modities chiefly exposed for sale in the public streets
are marine stores, hard-bake, apples, flat-fish, and
oysters." He observed that the streets presented
"a lively and animated appearance, occasioned chiefly
by the conviviality of the military." "The con-
sumption of tobacco in these towns," Mr. Pickwick
opined, "must be very great, and the smell which
pervades the streets must be exceedingly delicious to
those who are extremely fond of smoking. A super-
ficial traveller might object to the dirt, which is their
leading characteristic, but to those who view it as an
indication of traffic and commercial prosperity it is
truly gratifying." Were Mr. Pickwick to revisit
Chatham, he would find many of these characteristics
still prevailing, and could not fail to note, also, that
during the interval of more than sixty years the town
had undergone material changes in the direction of
modern improvements. When poor little David
Copperfield fled from his distressing experiences at
Murdstone and Grinby's, hoping to meet with a
welcome from Betsy Trotwood at Dover, he wended

* "The Mudfog Papers."
† Christmas Number of *Household Words*, 1854.

NORFOLK (NOW CLEVELAND) STREET, FITZROY SQUARE. (*Page 7.*)

Dickens and his parents resided in Norfolk Street in 1816, after their removal from Hawke Street, Portsea,

his weary way through Rochester; and as he toiled into Chatham, it seemed to him in the night's aspect "a mere dream of chalk, and drawbridges, and mastless ships in a muddy river, roofed like Noah's arks."[*]

Dickens himself, when a boy, must have seen the place frequently under similar conditions. The impressions he then received of Chatham and the neighbourhood were permanently fixed upon the mental retina, to be recalled again and again when penning his stories and descriptive pieces. In an article written by him in collaboration with Richard Hengist Horne, he supplies a picture of Chatham as it subsequently appeared when the military element on the main thoroughfares seemed paramount : " Men were only noticeable by scores, by hundreds, by thousands, rank and file, companies, regiments, detachments, vessels full for exportation. They walked about the streets in rows or bodies, carrying their heads in exactly the same way, and doing exactly the same thing with their limbs. Nothing in the shape of clothing was made for an individual, everything was contracted for by the millions. The children of Israel were established in Chatham, as salesmen, outfitters, tailors, old clothesmen, army and navy accoutrement makers, bill discounters, and general despoilers of the Christian world, in tribes rather than in families."[†]

John Dickens's official connection with the Navy Pay Department offered facilities for little Charles to roam unchecked about the busy dockyard, where he experienced delight in watching the ropemakers,

[*] " David Copperfield," chap. xiii.
[†] " One Man in a Dockyard " (*Household Words*, September 6, 1851).

anchor-smiths, and others at their labours, and in gazing with curious awe at the convict hulks (or prison ships), and where he found constant delight in observing the innumerable changes and variety of scenes ; on one day witnessing the bright display of military tactics on Chatham "Lines," on another enjoying a sail on the Medway with his father, when on duty bound for Sheerness in the Commissioners' yacht, a quaint, high-sterned sailing-vessel, pierced with circular ports, and dating from the seventeenth century ; she was broken up at Chatham in 1868.

The boy unconsciously stored up the pictures of life, and character, and scenery thus brought to his notice, to be recalled and utilized as valuable material by-and-bye. Of the great dockyard he afterwards wrote : " It resounded with the noise of hammers beating upon iron, and the great sheds or slips under which the mighty men-of-war are built loomed business-like when contemplated from the opposite side of the river. . . . Great chimneys smoking with a quiet—almost a lazy—air, like giants smoking tobacco; and the giant shears moored off it, looking meekly and inoffensively out of proportion, like the giraffe of the machinery creation."*

The famous Chatham Lines (constituting the fortifications of the town), are immortalized in " Pickwick " as the scene of the review at which Mr. Pickwick and his friends were present and got into difficulties; and the field adjacent to Fort Pitt (now the Chatham Military Hospital, standing on high ground near the railway station), was the locality selected for the intended duel between the irate

* " One Man in a Dockyard " (*Household Words*, September 6, 1851).

Dr. Slammer and the craven (but innocent) Mr. Winkle, both field and the contiguous land surrounding Fort Pitt being now a public recreation ground, whence is obtainable a fine panoramic view of Chatham and Rochester. The "Lines" are to-day locally understood as referring to an open space near Fort Pitt, which is used as an exercising ground for the soldiers at the barracks near by. All this portion of the country possessed great attractions for Dickens in later years; it was rendered familiar to him when, as a lad, he accompanied his father in walks about the locality, thus hallowed by old associations.

Ordnance Terrace, Chatham, retains much the same aspect it possessed at the time of John Dickens's residence there (1817-1821)—a row of three-storied houses, prominently situated on high ground within a short distance of the Chatham railway station. The Dickens abode was the second house in the terrace (now No. 11), whose front is now overgrown with a Virginia creeper, and so redeems its bareness. In describing the place, the late Mr. W. R. Hughes says: " It has the dining-room on the left-hand side of the entrance and the drawing-room on the first floor, and is altogether a pleasantly-situated, comfortable and respectable dwelling." At Ordnance Terrace, we are assured by Forster, it was that little Charles (" a very queer, small boy," as he afterwards described himself at this period) lived with his parents from his fifth to his ninth year; the child's " first desire for knowledge, and his greatest passion for reading, were awakened by his mother, who taught him the first rudiments, not only of English, but also, a little later, of Latin." The same authority states that he and his sister Fanny presently supplemented these home studies by attending a preparatory day-school in Rome Lane (now Railway Street), and that when revisiting Chatham in his manhood he tried to discover the place, found it had been pulled down "ages" before to make room for a new street; but there arose, nevertheless, "a not dim impression that it had been over a dyer's shop, that he went up steps to it, that he had frequently grazed his knees in doing so, and that, in trying to scrape the mud off a very unsteady little shoe, he generally got his leg over the scraper." Other recollections of the Ordnance Terrace days flashed upon him when engaged upon his "Boz" sketches; for example, the old lady in the sketch entitled "Our Parish" was drawn from a Mrs. Newnham who lived at No. 5 in the Terrace, and the original of the Half-Pay Captain (in the same sketch) was another near neighbour: at No. 1 there resided a winsome, golden-haired maiden named Lucy Stroughill, whom he regarded as his little sweetheart, and who figures as "Golden Lucy" in one of his Christmas stories,* while her brother George, "a frank, open, and somewhat daring boy," is believed to have inspired the creation of James Steerforth in "David Copperfield."

Little Charles must have been acquainted, too, with the prototype of Joe, the Fat Boy in "Pickwick," whose real name was James Budden, and whose father kept the Red Lion Inn at the corner of High Street and Military Road, Chatham, where the lad's remarkable obesity attracted general attention. The Mitre Inn and Clarence Hotel at Chatham, described

* "The Wreck of the Golden Mary" (Christmas Number of *Household Words*, 1856).

2 (NOW 11) ORDNANCE TERRACE, CHATHAM. (*Page 11.*)

Occupied by John Dickens and his family, 1817-1821.

in 1838 as "the first posting-house in the town," is also associated with Dickens's early years, and remains very much as it was when he knew it as a boy. At the period referred to the landlord of this fine old hostelry was a Mr. Tribe, with whose family Mr. and Mrs. John Dickens and their children were on visiting terms; indeed, it is recorded that, at the evening parties held at the Mitre, Charles distinguished himself by singing solos (usually old sea songs), and sometimes duets with his sister, both being mounted on a dining table for a stage. The Mitre is historically interesting by reason of the fact that Lord Nelson used to reside there when on duty at Chatham, a room he occupied being known as "Nelson's Cabin."*

In the eighteenth chapter of "The Mystery of Edwin Drood" we find the place disguised as "The Crozier"—"the orthodox hotel" at Cloisterham (i.e., Rochester)—and in "The Holly-Tree Inn" it is thus directly immortalized: "There was an inn in the cathedral town where I went to school, which had pleasanter recollections about it than any of these. . . . It was the inn where friends used to put up, and where we used to go and see parents, and to have salmon and fowls, and be tipped. It had an ecclesiastical sign—the Mitre—and a bar that seemed to be the next best thing to a bishopric, it was so snug."†

John Dickens had by nature a very generous

* See "The Guest" in the Christmas Number of *Household Words*, 1855.

† See "The Guest" in the Christmas Number of *Household Words*, 1855; Langton's "Childhood and Youth of Charles Dickens," 1883.

disposition, which inclined him to be too lavish in his expenditure. This idiosyncrasy, coupled with the ever-increasing demands of a young and growing family, compelled him to realize the immediate necessity for retrenchment. Hitherto his income (ranging from £200 to £350 per annum) amply sufficed to provide for the comfort of wife and children; but the time had arrived when rigid economy became imperative, and early in 1821 he removed into a less expensive and somewhat obscure habitation at No. 18, St. Mary's Place (otherwise called "The Brook"), Chatham, situated in the valley through which a brook (now covered over) flows into the Medway. The house on "The Brook," with a "plain-looking whitewashed plaster front, and a small garden before and behind," still exists; it is a semi-detached, six-roomed tenement, of a much humbler type than that in Ordnance Terrace, and stands next to what is now the Drill Hall of the Salvation Army, but which, in John Dickens's time, was a Baptist meeting-house called Providence Chapel. While the Dickens dwelling-place remains unaltered, the neighbourhood has since greatly deteriorated. The locality was then more rural and not so crowded as now, many of the people living there being of a quite respectable class. The minister then officiating at Providence Chapel was William Giles, whose son William had been educated at Oxford, and afterwards kept a school in Clover Lane (now Clover Street, the playground since covered by a railway station), Chatham, whence he moved to larger premises close by, still to be seen at the corner of Rhode Street and Best Street. Both Charles and his elder sister Fanny attended here as day scholars, and the boy, under Mr. Giles's able tuition, made rapid progress with his studies. Apropos of Mr. Giles, it should be mentioned that when his intelligent pupil had attained manhood and achieved fame as the author of "Pickwick," his old schoolmaster sent him, as a token of admiration, a silver snuff-box, the lid bearing an inscription addressed "To the Inimitable Boz." For a considerable time afterwards Dickens jocosely alluded to himself, in letters to intimate friends, as "the Inimitable." By the way, where is that snuff-box now?

St. Mary's Place is in close proximity to the old parish church of St. Mary, where the Dickens family worshipped during their residence in Chatham. It dates from the early part of the twelfth century, but having lately undergone a process of rebuilding, the edifice no longer possesses that quaintness which formerly characterized it, both externally and internally. The present structure, standing on a site which has been occupied by a church from Saxon times, has been erected from the designs of the late Sir Arthur Blomfield, already mentioned as the architect of the new parochial church of St. Mary, Kingston. Happily, there are preserved in St. Mary's, Chatham, some interesting remains of the Norman edifice (A.D. 1120), notably a fine doorway and staircase, and the columns of the central arch of the nave. Instead of the diminutive bell-turret originally surmounting the roof of the nave, a lofty detached tower now constitutes the most striking feature of the church, which was consecrated on October 28, 1903, in the presence of Lord Roberts. It has been suggested that the description of Blunderstone

Church in "David Copperfield" recalls in some respects the old parish church of Chatham, so familiar to Dickens in his boyhood, although the picture was partly drawn from Blundeston Church, Suffolk: "Here is our pew in the church. What a high-backed pew! with a window near it, out of which our house can be seen, and *is* seen many times during the morning's service by Peggotty, who likes to make herself as sure as she can that it's not being robbed, or is not in flames."* Dame Peggotty was no doubt to some extent depicted from Charles Dickens's nurse of those days, Mary Weller, who afterwards married Thomas Gibson, a shipwright in the dockyard, and whose death took place in 1888.

In the registers at Chatham Church are recorded the entries of the baptism of three children born in the parish to John and Elizabeth Dickens, the parents of the novelist; and Mary Allen, an aunt of Charles, was married by license there on December 11, 1821, to Dr. Lamert, a regimental surgeon, who afterwards figured in "Pickwick" as Dr. Slammer. In the church registers may be found several names subsequently used by Dickens in his stories—names of persons who lived in the district—Sowerby (Sowerberry), Tapley, Wren, Jasper, Weller, etc., the Tapleys and the Wellers being well-known cognomens, for there are vaults in the church belonging to the former family, and a gravestone in the churchyard erected to the latter. At the west end of the church there are two inscriptions to the family of Stroughill, who lived in Ordnance Terrace, and to whom reference has already been made. The Vicar, in his appeal for subscriptions in aid of the restora-

* "David Copperfield," chap. ii.

18 ST. MARY'S PLACE, THE BROOK, CHATHAM. (*Page* 14.)

tion fund, expressed a hope that the people of Chatham would contribute towards the cost of a memorial in the church to Charles Dickens. Apropos, I may mention that the Council of that flourishing institution the Dickens Fellowship have, very rightly, approached the Corporation of Chatham with the suggestion that they should place commemorative tablets on the two houses in Chatham in which he spent some of the happiest years of his boyhood, and the Corporation have consented.

From an upper window at the side of the house, No. 18, St. Mary's Place, an old graveyard was plainly visible, and frequently at night little Charles and his sister would gaze upon the God's-acre and at the heavens above from that point of vantage. Some thirty years later he recalled the circumstances in a poetical little story entitled "A Child's Dream of a Star,"* a touching reminiscence of these early days, where he says : "There was once a child, and he strolled about a good deal, and thought of a number of things. He had a sister, who was a child too, and his constant companion. These two used to wonder all day long. They wondered at the beauty of the flowers ; they wondered at the height and blueness of the sky ; they wondered at the depth of the bright water ; they wondered at the goodness and the power of God who made the lovely world.

"They used to say to one another sometimes, Supposing all the children upon earth were to die, would the flowers and the water and the sky be sorry ? They believed they would be sorry. For, said they, the buds are the children of the flowers, and the little playful streams that gambol down the

* *Household Words,* April 6, 1850.

hillsides are the children of the water, and the smallest bright specks playing at hide-and-seek in the sky all night must surely be the children of the stars; and they would all be grieved to see their playmates, the children of men, no more.

"There was one clear shining star that used to come out in the sky before the rest, near the church spire, above the graves. It was larger and more beautiful, they thought, than all the others, and every night they watched for it, standing hand in hand at a window. Whoever saw it first cried out, 'I see the star!' and often they cried out both together, knowing so well when it would rise, and where. So they grew to be such friends with it that, before lying down in their beds, they always looked out once again to bid it good-night ; and when they were turning round to sleep they used to say, 'God bless the star!'"

The Chatham days were replete with innocent delights for little Charles, whose young life over-flowed with the happiness resulting therefrom. He and his schoolfellows often went to see the sham fights and siege operations on the "Lines," and he enjoyed many a ramble with his sister and nurse in the fields about Fort Pitt ; and "the sky was so blue, the sun was so bright, the water was so spark-ling, the leaves were so green, the flowers were so lovely, and they heard such singing birds and saw so many butterflies, that everything was beautiful." In "The Child's Story," whence these extracts are culled, we find the following undoubted allusions to some of the juvenile pleasures in which the children indulged while at Chatham: "They had the merriest games that ever were played. . . . They had

FORT PITT, CHATHAM.   (*Page* 18.)

holidays, too, and 'twelfth-cakes,' and parties where
they danced till midnight, and real theatres, where
they saw palaces of real gold and silver rise out
of the real earth, and saw all the wonders of the
world at once. As to friends, they had such dear
friends and so many of them that I want the time to
reckon them up."* At home there were picture-
books and toys—"the finest toys in the world and
the most astonishing picture-books"—and, above all,
in the little room adjoining his bedchamber a small
library, consisting of the works of Fielding, Smollett,
Defoe, Goldsmith, the "Arabian Nights," and "Tales
of the Genii," which the boy perused with avidity
over and over again. "They kept alive my fancy,"
he said, as David Copperfield, "and my hope of
something beyond that place and time . . . and did
me no harm, for whatever harm was in some of
them was not there for me ; *I* knew nothing of it."†
In referring afterwards to the "readings" and "imaginations" which he described as brought away
from Chatham, he again observes with David : "The
picture always rises in my mind of a summer evening,
the boys at play in the churchyard, and I, sitting on
my bed, reading as if for life. Every barn in the
neighbourhood, every stone in the church, and every
foot of the churchyard, had some association of its
own in my mind connected with these books, and
stood for some locality made famous in them "‡—
words that were written down as fact some years
before they found their way into the story.

Happily for the boy, he remained in ignorance of

---

* *Household Words*, Christmas Number, 1852.
† "David Copperfield," chap. iv.
‡ *Ibid.*

the changes impending at home, and unconscious of
the fact that he was about to relinquish for ever the
delectations afforded by those daily visions of his
childhood ; the ships on the Medway, the military
paradings and manœuvres, the woods and pastures,
the delightful walks with his father to Rochester and
Cobham—all were to vanish, as Forster says, " like a
dream"; for in 1822 John Dickens was recalled
to Somerset House, and in the winter of that year
he departed by coach for London, accompanied by
his wife and children, excepting Charles, who was left
behind for a few weeks longer in the care of the
worthy schoolmaster, William Giles. Presently the
day arrived when the lonesome lad followed his
parents to the Metropolis, leaving behind him, alas !
everything that gave his " ailing little life its
picturesqueness or sunshine "; for he was really a
very sickly boy, and for that reason unable to join
with zest in the more vigorous sports of his play-
fellows, which explains his fondness for reading,
so unusual in lads of his age.

Little Charles was only ten years old when he
bade farewell to Chatham, and took his place as a
passenger in the stage-coach " Commodore." " There
was no other inside passenger," he afterwards observed, " and I consumed my sandwiches in solitude
and dreariness, and it rained hard all the way, and I
thought life sloppier than I expected to find it."
Like Philip Pirrip, he might with more justice have
thought that henceforth he " was for London and
greatness."   Undoubtedly he experienced the same
sensations as those of that youthful hero who, under
similar circumstances, realized that " all beyond was
so unknown and great that in a moment with a

strong heave and sob I broke into tears."* Reminiscences of that memorable journey are recorded
in one of that charming series of papers contributed
by him to *All the Year Round* under the general
title of "The Uncommercial Traveller." Dickens
here calls his boyhood's home "Dullborough"—
"most of us come from Dullborough who come
from a country town"—informing us that as he left
the place "in the days when there were no railways
in the land," he left it in a stage-coach, and further
takes us into his confidence by saying that he had
never forgotten, nor lost the smell of, the damp straw
in which he was packed, "like game, and forwarded,
carriage paid, to the Cross Keys, Wood Street,
Cheapside, London." These words were written in
June, 1860, and a few months later, when penning
the twentieth chapter of "Great Expectations," he
again recalled the episode: "The journey from our
town to the Metropolis was a journey of about five
hours. It was a little past mid-day when the four-
horse stage-coach by which I was a passenger got
into the ravel of traffic frayed out about the Cross
Keys, Wood Street, Cheapside, London. . . . The
coach that had carried me away was melodiously
called 'Timpson's Blue-Eyed Maid,' and belonged to
Timpson, at the coach-office up-street. . . . Timpson's was a moderate-sized coach-office (in fact, a
little coach-office), with an oval transparency in the
window, which looked beautiful by night, representing
one of Timpson's coaches in the act of passing a
milestone on the London road with great velocity,
completely full inside and out, and all the passengers
dressed in the first style of fashion, and enjoying

* "Great Expectations," chap. xix.

themselves tremendously." He found, on a later visit to Rochester and Chatham, that Timpson's had disappeared, for "Pickford had come and knocked Timpson's down," and "had knocked two or three houses down on each side of Timpson's, and then had knocked the whole into one great establishment. . . ."* The late Mr. Robert Langton states that Timpson was really Simpson (the coach proprietor at Chatham), and that the "Blue-Eyed Maid" was a veritable coach, to which reference is also made in the third chapter of "Little Dorrit."

If, as Forster tells us, the "Commodore," and not the "Blue-Eyed Maid," conveyed little Charles to London, it was the identical vehicle by which Mr. Pickwick and his companions travelled from the Golden Cross at Charing Cross to Rochester, as duly set forth in the opening chapter of "The Pickwick Papers"; this coach was driven by old Cholmeley (or Chumley), who is said to have been the original of Tony Weller, and concerning whom some amusing anecdotes are related in "Nimrod's Northern Tour."

* *All the Year Round*, June 30, 1860.

THE GOLDEN CROSS, CHARING CROSS, CIRCA 1827. (*Page 22.*)

Showing the hotel as it was in the Pickwickian days.

From a print in the collection of Councillor Newton, Hampstead.

CHAPTER II.

BOYHOOD AND YOUTH IN LONDON.

IT was in the early spring of 1823 that Charles Dickens made acquaintance with London for the second time, that vast Metropolis which henceforth continued to exercise a fascination over him, and in the study of which, as well as of its various types of humanity, he found a perpetual charm. His early impressions, however, were not of the brightest, having (as he subsequently observed) exchanged "everything that had given his ailing little life its picturesqueness or sunshine" for the comparatively sordid environment of a London suburb, and suffered the deprivation of the companionship of his play-fellows at Chatham to become a solitary lad under circumstances that could not fail to make sorrowful the stoutest heart, not the least depressing being his father's money involvement with consequent poverty at home. John Dickens, whose financial affairs demanded retrenchment, had rented what Forster describes as "a mean, small tenement" at No. 16 (now No. 141), Bayham Street, Camden Town, to-day one of the poorest parts of London, but not quite so wretched then as we are led to suppose by the reference in Forster's biography. The cottages in Bayham Street, built in 1812, were comparatively

new in 1823, and then stood in the midst of what may be regarded as rural surroundings, there being a meadow at the back of the principal row of houses, in which haymaking was carried on in its season, while a beautiful walk across the fields led to Copenhagen House. Dickens averred that "a washerwoman lived next door" to his father, and "a Bow Street officer lived over the way." We learn, too, that at the top of the street were some almshouses, and when revisiting the spot many years later Dickens told his biographer that "to go to this spot and look from it over the dust-heaps and dockleaves and fields at the cupola of St. Paul's looming through the smoke was a treat that served him for hours of vague reflection afterwards." A writer who vividly remembered Camden Town as it appeared when John Dickens lived there has placed upon record some interesting particulars concerning it. He says : " In the days I am referring to gas was unknown. We had little twinkling oil-lamps. As soon as it became dark, the watchman went his rounds, starting from his box at the north end of Bayham Street, against the tea - gardens of the Mother Red Cap, then a humble roadside house, kept by a widow and her two daughters, of the name of Young. Then the road between Kentish and Camden Towns was very lonely—hardly safe after dark. These certainly were drawbacks, for depredations used frequently to be committed in the back premises of the houses. . . . The nearest church was Old St. Pancras, then in the midst of fields." *
Exception has been taken to Forster's use of the

* _Vide_ " St. Pancras, Past and Present," by Frederick Muller, 1874.

16 (NOW 141) BAYHAM STREET, CAMDEN TOWN.   (*Page* 24).

Dickens and his parents lived here in 1823. The house was also the residence of
Mr. Micawber, and the district is mentioned in " Dombey and Son"
under the name of Staggs Gardens.

word "squalid" as applied to the Bayham Street of 1823, and with justification, for persons of some standing made it their abode, and we learn that in certain of the twenty or thirty newly-erected houses there lived Engelhart and Francis Holl, the celebrated engravers, the latter the father of Frank Holl, the Royal Academician ; Charles Rolls and Henry Selous, artists of note ; and Angelo Selous, the dramatic author. Thus it would appear that Bayham Street, during the early part of its history, was eminently respectable, and we are compelled to presume that Dickens's unfavourable presentment of the locality was the outcome of his own painful environment, such as would be forcibly impressed upon the mind of a sickly child (as he then was) and one keenly susceptible to outward influences. Undoubtedly, as Forster remarks, "he felt crushed and chilled by the change from the life at Chatham, breezy and full of colour, to the little back garret in Bayham Street," and, looking upon the dingy brick tenement to-day, it is not difficult to realize this fact ; for, although the house itself could not have been less attractive than his previous home on "the Brook" at Chatham, the surroundings did not offer advantages in the shape of country walks and riverside scenery such as the immediate neighbourhood of Chatham afforded.*

* To Mr. R. B. Prosser (editor of *St. Pancras Notes and Queries*) I am indebted for much useful information respecting the early London homes of Charles Dickens. He has discovered that in the parish rate-book for October 8, 1823, the name of John Dickens appears as the tenant of No. 16, Bayham Street, and also at No. 18; in the next rate-book (January 21, 1824) No. 16 is marked "empty." In 1866 the Metropolitan Board of Works renumbered Bayham Street (then consisting of about a hundred and fifty houses), incorporating therewith Bayham Street South and Fleming Place.

Bayham Street was named after Bayham Abbey in Sussex, one of the seats of the Marquis Camden. Eighty years ago this part of suburban London was but a village, and Bayham Street had grass struggling through the newly-paved road. Thus we are forced to the conclusion that the misery and depression of spirits, from which little Charles suffered while living here, must be attributed to family adversity and his own isolated condition rather than to the character of his environment. At this time his father's pecuniary resources became so circumscribed as to compel the observance of the strictest domestic economy, and prevented him from continuing his son's education. "As I thought," said Dickens on one occasion very bitterly, "in the little back-garret in Bayham Street, of all I had lost in losing Chatham, what would I have given—if I had had anything to give—to have been sent back to any other school, to have been taught something anywhere!"

Instead of improving, the elder Dickens's affairs grew from bad to worse, and all ordinary efforts to propitiate his creditors having been exhausted, Mrs. Dickens laudably resolved to attempt a solution of the difficulty by means of a school for young ladies. Accordingly, a house was taken at No. 4, Gower Street North, whither the family removed in 1823. This and the adjoining houses had only just been built. The rate-book shows that No. 4 was taken in the name of Mrs. Dickens, at an annual rental of £50, and that it was in the occupation of the Dickens family from Michaelmas, 1823, to Lady Day, 1824, they having apparently left Bayham Street at Christmas of the former year. No. 4, Gower Street North stood a little to the north of Gower Street

Chapel, erected in 1820, and still existing on the west side of the road ; the house, known in recent times as No. 147, Gower Street, was demolished about 1895, and an extension of Messrs. Maple's premises now occupies the site. When, in 1890, I visited the place with my friend the late Mr. W. R. Hughes (author of " A Week's Tramp in Dickens Land "), we found it in the occupation of a manufacturer of artificial human eyes, a sort of Mr. Venus, with his " human eyes warious," as depicted in " Our Mutual Friend"; while there was a dancing academy next door, reminiscent of Mr. Turveydrop, the professor of deportment in " Bleak House." The Dickens residence had six small rooms, with kitchen in basement, each front room having two windows—altogether a fairly comfortable abode, but minus a garden. The result of Mrs. Dickens's enterprise proved as disastrous as that of Mrs. Micawber's. " Poor Mrs. Micawber ! She said she had tried to exert herself ; and so, I have no doubt, she had. The centre of the street door was perfectly covered with a great brass plate, on which was engraved, ' Mrs. Micawber's Boarding Establishment for Young Ladies'; but I never found that any young ladies had ever been to school there ; or that any young lady ever came, or proposed to come ; or that the least preparation was ever made to receive any young lady." The actual facts are thus recorded in fiction, and the futility of Mrs. Dickens's excellent intention to retrieve the family misfortunes seemed inevitable, in spite of the energy displayed by the youthful Charles in distributing " at a great many doors a great many circulars," calling attention to the superior advantages of the new seminary. The blow proved a crushing one, rendering the prospect more hopeless than ever. Importunate creditors, who could no longer be kept at bay, effected the arrest of John Dickens, who was conveyed forthwith to a prison for debtors in the Borough of Southwark ; his last words to his heart-broken son as he was carried off being similar to those despondingly uttered by Mr. Micawber under like circumstances, to the effect that the sun was set upon him for ever.

Forster says that the particular prison where John Dickens suffered incarceration was the Marshalsea, and this statement appears correct, judging from the fragment of the novelist's autobiography which refers to the unfortunate incident : " And he told me, I remember, to take warning by the Marshalsea, and to observe that if a man had twenty pounds a year, and spent nineteen pounds nineteen shillings and sixpence, he would be happy ; but that a shilling spent the other way would make him wretched." Another of Mr. Micawber's wise sayings, be it observed. That impecunious gentleman (it will be remembered) suffered imprisonment at the King's Bench, and it may be surmised that the novelist purposely changed the locale that old memories should not be revived. Of debtors' prisons considerable knowledge is displayed in his books, his personal acquaintance with them dating, of course, from those days when the brightness of his young life was obscured by the "falling cloud" to which he compares this distressing time. Realistic and accurate pictures of the most noteworthy of these blots upon our social system may be found in the forcible description in the fortieth chapter of "Pickwick" of the Fleet Prison, of which the last vestiges were removed in 1872, and the site of which is now covered by the Memorial Hall, Farringdon Street, and by Messrs. Cassell and Co.'s printing works; the King's Bench Prison (long since demolished) figures prominently in "David Copperfield"; while many of the principal scenes in "Little Dorrit" are laid in the departed Marshalsea, which adjoined the burial-ground of St. George's Church in the Borough. The extreme rear of the Marshalsea Prison, described by Dickens in the preface to "Little Dorrit," was transformed into a warehouse in 1887.

The second chapter of Forster's biography makes dismal reading, relating, as it does, the bitter experiences of Charles Dickens's boyhood—experiences, however, which yielded abundant material for future use in his stories. With the breadwinner in the clutches of the law, the wife and children, left stranded in the Gower Street house, had a terrible struggle for existence; we are told that in order to obtain the necessaries of life their bits of furniture and various domestic utensils were pawned or otherwise disposed of, until at length the place was practically emptied of its contents, and the inmates were perforce compelled to encamp in the two parlours, living there night and day. At this juncture a relative, James Lamert (who had lodged with the family in Bayham Street), heard of their misfortunes, and, through his connection with Warren's Blacking Manufactory at 30, Hungerford Stairs, Strand, provided an occupation there for little Charles by which he could earn a few shillings a week—a miserable pittance, but extremely welcome under the circumstances, as, by exercising strict economy, it enabled him to support himself, thus making one mouth less to provide for at home. Hungerford Stairs (in after-life he used to declare that he knew *Hunger*-ford well!) stood near the present Charing Cross railway bridge (which usurps the old Hungerford Suspension Bridge, transferred to Clifton), and the site of Hungerford Market is covered by the railway station. Dickens has recorded that "the blacking warehouse was the last house on the left-hand side of the way, at old Hungerford Stairs. It was a crazy, tumble-down old house, abutting, of course, on the river, and literally overrun with rats. Its wainscotted rooms and its rotten floors and staircase, and the old grey rats swarming down in the cellars, and the sound of their squeaking and scuffling coming up the stairs at all times, and the dirt and decay of the place, rise up vividly before me, as if I were there again." The blacking factory, which disappeared when Hungerford Market went, is faithfully portrayed in the eleventh chapter of "David Copperfield," thinly disguised as Murdstone and Grinby's Warehouse, "down in Blackfriars." Dickens, like David, was keenly sensible of the humiliation of what he could not help regarding as a very menial occupation—the tying-up and labelling innumerable pots of paste-blacking—which he was now destined to follow, and for the remainder of his life he never recalled this episode without a pang.

He reminded Forster how fond he was of roaming about the neighbourhood of the Strand and Covent Garden during the dinner hour, intently observing the various types of humanity with precocious interest, and storing up impressions which were destined to prove invaluable to him. One of his favourite localities was the Adelphi, and he was particularly attracted by a little waterside tavern called the Fox-under-the-Hill; doubtless the incident narrated in the just-mentioned chapter of " Copperfield "—the autobiographical chapter — is true of himself, when he causes little David to confess to a fondness for wandering about that " mysterious place with those dark arches," and to wonder what the coalheavers thought of him, a solitary lad, as he sat upon a bench outside the little public-house, watching them as they danced.* The pudding-shops and beef-houses in the neighbourhood of St. Martin's Lane and Drury Lane were familiar enough to him in those days ; for, with such a modest sum to invest for his mid-day meal, he naturally compared notes as to the charges made by each for a slice of pudding or cold spiced beef before deciding upon the establishment which should have the privilege of his custom. He sometimes favoured Johnson's in Clare Court, which is identical with the place patronized by David Copperfield—viz., the " famous alamode beef-house near Drury Lane," where he gave the waiter a half-penny, and wished he hadn't taken it. In the recently demolished Clare Court there existed in those days two of the best alamode beef-shops in London, the Old Thirteen Cantons and the New Thirteen Cantons, and we read in a curious

* The Fox-under-the-Hill stood at the foot of Ivy Bridge Lane, which formed a boundary between Westminster City and the Liberty of the Duchy of Lancaster (Savoy). Between Salisbury Stairs (adjoining the little tavern) and London Bridge there plied three halfpenny steamboats, named respectively the *Ant*, the *Bee*, and the *Cricket*, whereof the latter two came to an untimely end. The building of the Hotel Cecil has wiped out Cecil and Salisbury Streets, and entirely transformed this locality, including the destruction of the quaint ale-house itself.

book called " The Epicure's Almanack " (1815), that " the beef and liquors at either house are equally good, and the attention of all who pass is attracted by the display of fine sallads in the windows, which display is daily executed with great ingenuity, and comprehends a variety of neat devices, in which the fine slices of red beetroot are pleasingly conspicuous." The New Thirteen Cantons was kept by the veritable Johnson himself. We are further informed that he owned a clever dog called Carlo, " who once enacted so capital a part on the boards of Old Drury," and whose sagacity " brought as many customers to Mr. Johnson as did the excellence of his fare." Dickens, however, did not become acquainted with Carlo, who, a few years before the lad knew the shop, paid the penalty of a report that the famous animal had been bitten by a mad dog. " There were two pudding-shops," said Dickens to his biographer, " between which I was divided, according to my finances." One was in a court close to St. Martin's Church, where the pudding was made with currants, " and was rather a special pudding," but dear ; the other was in the Strand, " somewhere in that part which has been rebuilt since," where the pudding was much cheaper, being stout and pale, heavy and flabby, with a few big raisins stuck in at great distances apart. The more expensive shop stood in Church Court (at the back of the church), demolished when Adelaide Street was constructed about 1830, and may probably be identified with the Oxford eating-house, then existing opposite the departed Hungerford Street ; the other establishment, where Dickens often dined for economy's sake, flourished near the spot covered until quite recently by that

DICKENS AT THE BLACKING WAREHOUSE. *(Page 29.)*

*From a drawing by Fred Barnard. Reproduced by kind permission of
Messrs. Chapman and Hall.*

children's paradise, the Lowther Arcade. The courts surrounding St. Martin's Church were formerly so thronged with eating-houses that the district became popularly known as " Porridge Island."

Failing, by means of a certain "deed," to propitiate his creditors, John Dickens continued to remain within the gloomy walls of the Marshalsea. The home in Gower Street was thereupon broken up, and Mrs. Dickens, with her family, went to live with her husband in the prison. Little Charles, however, was handed over as a lodger to a Mrs. Roylance, a reduced old lady who afterwards figured as Mrs. Pipchin in " Dombey and Son." Mrs. Roylance, long known to the family, resided in Little College Street, Camden Town ; it became College Street West in 1828, and the portion north of King Street has been known since 1887 as College Place. The abode in question was probably No. 37, for, according to the rate-book of 1824 (the period with which I am dealing), the house so numbered (rated at £18) was occupied by Elizabeth *Raylase** until the following year, and demolished about 1890, at which time the street was rebuilt.

The boy still carried on his uncongenial duties at the blacking warehouse with satisfaction to his employers, in spite of the acute mental suffering he underwent. Experiencing a sense of loneliness in being cut off from his parents, brothers, and sisters, he pleaded to his father to be allowed to lodge nearer the prison, with the result that he left Mrs. Roylance, to take up his abode in Lant Street, Borough, where, in the house of an insolvent court agent, a back attic

* Possibly a mistake of the rate-collector. The name Roylance is not uncommon in the district.

had been found for him, having from the little window "a pleasant prospect of a timber-yard." Of Lant Street, as it probably then appeared, we have a capital description in the thirty-second chapter of the " Pickwick Papers," for here it was that Bob Sawyer found a lodgment with the amiable (!) Mrs. Raddle and her husband, in the identical house, maybe, as that tenanted by the insolvent court agent. "There is a repose about Lant Street, in the Borough, which sheds a gentle melancholy upon the soul. There are always a good many houses to let in the street ; it is a by-street, too, and its dulness is soothing. A house in Lant Street would not come within the denomination of a first-rate residence in the strict acceptation of the term, but it is a most desirable spot, nevertheless. If a man wished to abstract himself from the world, to remove himself from within the reach of temptation, to place himself beyond the possibility of any inducement to look out of the window, he should by all means go to Lant Street.

" In this happy retreat are colonized a few clear-starchers, a sprinkling of journeymen bookbinders, one or two prison agents for the insolvent court, several small housekeepers who are employed in the docks, a handful of mantua-makers, and a seasoning of jobbing tailors. The majority of the inhabitants either direct their energies to the letting of furnished apartments, or devote themselves to the healthful and invigorating pursuit of mangling. The chief features in the still life of the street are green shutters, lodging-bills, brass door-plates, and bell-handles, the principal specimens of animated nature, the pot-boy, the muffin youth, and the baked-potato man. The

LANT STREET, BOROUGH. (*Page* 34.)

Showing the older residential tenements.   The actual house in which Dickens lived as a boy is
now demolished.

population is migratory, usually disappearing on the verge of quarter-day, and generally by night. His Majesty's revenues are seldom collected in this happy valley ; the rents are dubious, and the water communication is very frequently cut off."

Lant Street, as Bob Sawyer informed Mr. Pickwick, is near Guy's Hospital, "little distance after you've passed St. George's Church—turns out of the High Street on the right-hand side of the way." It has not altered materially in its outward aspect since the time when little Charles Dickens slept there, on the floor of the back attic, an abode which he then thought was "a paradise." We may suppose that such accommodation, poor as it must have been, yielded some consolation to the lonely child by reason of the fact that he was within easy reach of his parents, and also because his landlord—a fat, good-natured old gentleman, who was lame—and his quiet old wife were very kind to him ; and it is interesting to know that they and their grown-up son are immortalized in "The Old Curiosity Shop" as the Garland family. Little Charles looked forward to Saturday nights, when his release from toil at an earlier hour than usual enabled him to indulge his fancy for rambling and loitering a little in the busy thoroughfares between Hungerford Stairs and the Marshalsea. His usual way home was over Blackfriars Bridge, and then to the left along Charlotte Street, which (he is careful to tell us) "has Rowland Hill's chapel on one side, and the likeness of a golden dog licking a golden pot over a shop door on the other," a quaint sign still existing here. He was sometimes tempted to expend a penny to enter a show-van which generally stood at a corner of the street "to see the fat pig, the wild Indian, and the little lady," and for long afterwards could recall the peculiar smell of hat-making then (and now) carried on there.

The autobiographical record discloses another characteristic incident, which was afterwards embodied in the eleventh chapter of " Copperfield."

One evening little Charles had acted as messenger for his father at the Marshalsea, and was returning to the prison by way of Westminster Bridge, when he went into a public-house in Parliament Street, at the corner of Derby Street, and ordered a glass of the *very best* ale (the " Genuine Stunning "), "with a good head to it." " The landlord," observes Dickens, " looked at me, in return, over the bar from head to foot, with a strange smile on his face ; and instead of drawing the beer, looked round the screen and said something to his wife, who came out from behind it, with her work in her hand, and joined him in surveying me. Here we stand, all three, before me now, in my study at Devonshire Terrace—the landlord in his shirt-sleeves, leaning against the bar window-frame, his wife looking over the little half-door, and I, in some confusion, looking up at them from outside the partition. They asked me a good many questions, as what my name was, how old I was, where I lived, how I was employed, etc., etc. To all of which, that I might commit nobody, I invented appropriate answers. They served me with the ale, though I expect it was not the strongest on the premises ; and the landlord's wife, opening the little half-door and bending down, gave me a kiss that was half-admiring and half-compassionate, but all womanly and good." I am sure "so juvenile a customer was evidently unusual at the Red Lion"; and he explains that "the occasion was a festive one," either his own birthday or somebody else's, but I doubt whether this would prove sufficient justification in the eyes of the rigid total abstainer. In "David Copperfield" we find an illustration of the scene depicted in a clever etching by "Phiz." The public-house here referred to is the Red Lion, which has been lately rebuilt, and differs considerably from the unpretentious tavern as Dickens knew it; unfortunately, the sign of the rampant red lion has not been replaced, but in its stead we see a bust of the novelist, standing within a niche in the principal front of the new building.

By a happy stroke of good fortune, a rather considerable legacy from a relative accrued to John Dickens, and had been paid into court during his incarceration. This, in addition to the official pension due for long service at Somerset House, enabled him to meet his financial responsibilities, with the result that the Marshalsea knew him no more. Just then, too, the blacking business had become larger, and was transferred to Chandos Street, Covent Garden, where little Charles continued to manipulate the pots, but in a more public manner; for here the work was done in a window facing the street, and generally in the presence of an admiring crowd outside. The warehouse (pulled down in 1889) stood next to the shop at the corner of Bedford Street in Chandos Street (the southern corner, now the Civil Service Stores); opposite, there was the public-house where the lad got his ale. "The stones on the street," he afterwards observed to Forster, "may be smoothed by my small feet going across to it at dinner-time, and back again." The basement of the warehouse became transformed in later years into a chemist's shop, and the sign of the tavern over the way was the Black Prince, closed in 1888, and demolished shortly afterwards to make room for buildings devoted to the medical school of the Charing Cross Hospital. His release from prison compelled the elder Dickens to seek another abode for himself and family, and he obtained temporary quarters with the before-mentioned Mrs. Roylance of Little College Street. Thence, according to Forster, they went to Hampstead, where the elder Dickens had taken a house, and from there, in 1825, he removed to a small tenement in Johnson Street, Somers Town, a poverty-stricken neighbourhood even in those days, and changed but little since. Johnson Street was then the last street in Somers Town, and adjoined the fields between it and Camden Town. It runs east from the north end of Seymour Street, and the house occupied by the Dickens family (including Charles, who had, of course, left his Lant Street "paradise") was No. 13, at the east end of the north side, if we may rely upon the evidence afforded by the rate-book. At that time the house was numbered 29, and rated at £20, the numbering being changed to 13 at Christmas, 1825. In July of that year the name of the tenant is entered in the rate-book as Caroline Dickens, and so remains until January, 1829, after which the house is marked "Empty."

Brighter days were in store for the Dickens family, and especially for little Charles, whose father could now afford to send him to a good school in the neighbourhood, much to the boy's delight. Owing

THE SIGN OF THE DOG'S HEAD IN THE POT, CHARLOTTE STREET,
BLACKFRIARS. (*Page* 35.)

" That turning in the Blackfriars Road which has Rowland Hill's Chapel on one side, and the
likeness of a golden dog licking a golden pot over a shop door at the other " (Forster).

to a quarrel (of which he was the subject) between John Dickens and James Lamert, the father declared that his boy should leave the blacking warehouse and go to school instead. Thus terminated, suddenly and unexpectedly, that period of his life which Charles Dickens ever regarded with a feeling of repugnance. "Until old Hungerford Market was pulled down," he tells us, "until old Hungerford Stairs were destroyed, and the very nature of the ground changed, I never had the courage to go back to the place where my servitude began." He never saw it, and could not endure to go near it, and, in order that a certain smell of the cement used for putting on the blacking-corks should not revive unpleasant associations, he would invariably, when approaching Warren's later establishment in Chandos Street, cross over to the opposite side of the way.

He was about twelve years of age when he and the blacking-pots parted company for ever, and the new and more promising prospect opened before him—a future replete with possibilities, and yielding opportunities of which he knew the value and made the best use. The school to which he was sent as a day-scholar was called the Wellington House Academy, the proprietor being a Welshman named William Jones, whose "classical and commercial" seminary stood at the north-east corner of Granby Street, Hampstead Road. The residential portion still exists, although doomed to early demolition; but the detached schoolroom and large playground disappeared in 1835, on the formation of the London and Birmingham Railway, as it was then called. In a paper entitled "Our School," contributed to *Household Words* in 1851, Dickens gives a thinly-veiled account of Jones's Academy, and those of his pupils who yet survive readily understand the various allusions, and vouch for the general accuracy of the presentment. " It was a school," he says, " of some celebrity in its neighbourhood—nobody could say why ; the master was supposed among us to know nothing, and one of the ushers was supposed to know everything." There can be no doubt that Wellington House Academy and its proprietor are revived in " David Copperfield " as Salem House and Mr. Creakle.

The most accessible route for young Dickens to follow between his home in Johnson Street and the school was by way of Drummond Street, then a quiet semi-rural thoroughfare, bounded on the north side by the cow pastures belonging to an ancestor of the late Cecil Rhodes (of South African fame), many members of whose family were located here. Dr. Dawson, a schoolfellow of Dickens at Wellington House, well remembered him acting as ringleader of other lads, and, simulating poverty, imploring charity from people in Drummond Street, especially old ladies.

Among other associations of the future novelist with this locality may be mentioned his attendance (in company with Dr. Dawson) at the Sunday morning services in Somers Chapel (now called St. Mary's Parish Church), in Seymour Street (then partly fields), Somers Town,* concerning which act of piety Dr. Dawson regrets to observe that his lively and irreverent young friend "did not attend in the slightest degree to the service, but incited me

* In 1820 Seymour Street, with the site of Euston Square Station, was a huge brick-field, with a solitary "wine vaults" stuck in the middle of it.

29 (NOW 13) JOHNSON STREET, SOMERS TOWN. (*Page* 38.)

The home of Dickens in 1824.

to laughter by declaring his dinner was ready, and the potatoes would be spoiled, and, in fact, behaved in such a manner that it was lucky for us we were not ejected from the chapel." He remained at Wellington House Academy about two years (1824-1826), without achieving any particular distinction as a pupil. Thus ended his school training, elementary at the best, and it has been truly observed that a classical education might have "done for" him—that "Boz," like Burns, might have acquired all necessary erudition in a Board school. "Pray, Mr. Dickens, where was your son educated?" conjured a friend of John Dickens, who significantly and pertinently replied, "Why, indeed, sir—ha! ha! —he may be said to have educated himself!" a response which the novelist used good-humouredly and whimsically to imitate in Forster's hearing.

On relinquishing his studies at the age of fourteen, Charles Dickens for a brief period was installed as clerk in the service of Mr. Molloy, a solicitor in New Square, Lincoln's Inn. His father, however, presently transferred him to the offices of Messrs. Ellis and Blackmore, attorneys, at No. 1, Raymond Buildings, Gray's Inn (second floor), the clerks' office looking out upon the roadway ; here he performed similar duties from May, 1827, to November, 1828, at a weekly salary of 13s. 6d., rising to 15s. Although he did not relish the law, and failed to appreciate the particular kind of responsibility devolving upon him as a humble apprentice to that profession, the few months thus employed by him were productive of fruitful results, for they afforded him opportunities of studying the idiosyncrasies of lawyers, their clerks and clients, which can only be obtained by intimate

8

association. In the words of David Copperfield, he said: "I looked at nothing that I know of, but I saw everything," with the result that he culled from his mental storehouse those vivid pictures of legal life and character as portrayed in "The Pickwick Papers," "Sketches by Boz," and later works. The Dickens family at this time had left the unattractive environment of Johnson Street and made their home at the Polygon, Somers Town, a much more respectable and refined quarter, where Harold Skimpole (in "Bleak House") afterwards settled, and "where there were at that time a number of poor Spanish refugees walking about in cloaks, smoking little paper cigars." The Polygon was so called from the arrangement of the houses in the form of a circle; it stood within Clarendon Square, and, on completion, became the aristocratic part of Somers Town; many successful artists and engravers selecting it as a place of residence.* The name of Dickens, however, does

* A writer in Hone's "Year-Book," 1826, says: "Somers Town is full of artists, as a reference to the Royal Academy Catalogue will evince. In Clarendon Square still lives, I believe, Scriven, the engraver, an artist of great ability and, in his day, of much consideration. In the same neighbourhood dwells the venerable Dr. Wilde, who may be justly termed the best engraver of his age for upwards of half a century."

W. H. Wills (assistant editor on *All the Year Round*), in recalling Somers Town of this period, refers to its "aristocracy," and to the Polygon as its "Court centre," situated in the middle of Clarendon Square. "In and around it," he says, "Art and Literature nestled in cosy coteries, with half-pay officers (including one Peninsular Colonel), city merchants, and stock-brokers. . . . The most eminent historical engravers of that day dated their works, 'as the Act directs,' from Somers Town." Theodore Hook lived in Clarendon Square, and Peter Pindar, Sir Francis Burdett, with other notabilities, in close proximity thereto.

WELLINGTON HOUSE ACADEMY, HAMPSTEAD ROAD. (*Page* 39.)

not appear in the contemporary rate-book, but we find recorded there the significant fact that No. 17 was then " let to lodgers "—a very unusual entry— and this, added to the fact that the rents were comparatively high, justifies the assumption that the Dickens family were lodgers only at the house bearing that number. At this time John Dickens, with commendable energy and perseverance, had acquired the difficult art of shorthand writing, with a view to obtaining a livelihood as a Parliamentary reporter. He apparently changed his address with some frequency, in 1832-1833 living for a time at Highgate, whither Charles accompanied him, and lodging during brief intervals in the western part of London. Certain letters written by the son to an intimate friend indicate such addresses as North End (? Fulham) and Fitzroy Street.

The father, on securing an appointment as a reporter for the *Morning Herald*, established himself and his family (including Charles), at No. 18, Bentinck Street, Manchester Square. The rate-book, however, does not give his name as the tenant of this or any other house in the street, so we must assume that the family were again merely lodgers. This house and its neighbours were recently demolished, being replaced by a row of mansions, and, oddly enough, the name of the occupier of No. 19 in 1895 bore the novelist's patronymic.

On leaving Ellis and Blackmore's office in Novem-

The houses which comprised the Polygon prior to 1890 were demolished by the Midland Railway Company in the following year, and the buildings now occupying the site were erected by the Company for habitation by persons of the labouring class who were displaced by the acquisition of the property.

ber, 1828, Charles Dickens abandoned the pursuit of
the law for ever.

The profession of journalism offering him superior
attractions, he was tempted to become a newspaper
reporter.   With that object in view, he gave himself
up to the study of stenography, devoting much of
his time at the British Museum acquiring a knowledge of the subject, and practising in the Law Courts
of Doctors' Commons with extraordinary assiduity
until he arrived at something like proficiency.   The
impediments that beset him are duly set forth in the
pages of "David Copperfield," the incidents there
narrated being based upon the author's heart-breaking
experience in endeavouring to master the mysteries
of shorthand.   Like David, he passed a period of
probation, lasting nearly two years, reporting for the
Proctors at Doctors' Commons, St. Paul's Churchyard.   The scene of his labours is thus described in
"Sketches by Boz": "Crossing a quiet and shady
courtyard paved with stone, and frowned upon by
old red-brick houses, on the doors of which were
painted the names of sundry learned civilians, we
paused before a small, green-baized, brass-headed
nailed door, which, yielding to our gentle push, at
once admitted us into an old quaint-looking apartment, with sunken windows and black carved wains-
cotting, at the upper end of which, seated on a raised
platform of semicircular shape, were about a dozen
solemn-looking gentlemen in crimson gowns and
wigs."   The courts were destroyed in 1867, and in
their place a Royal Court of Probate was established
at Westminster Hall.

According to the autographs on certain British
Museum readers' slips, Charles Dickens was residing,

in 1831, at No. 10, Norfolk Street, Fitzroy Square, the same street (now Cleveland Street, east side of Middlesex Hospital) in which his father was domiciled for a while in 1814.

About the year 1833 Charles rented bachelor apartments in Cecil Street (Strand), as evidenced by a letter of that period to an intimate friend, where he says : " The people at Cecil Street put too much water in the hashes, lost the nutmeg-grater, attended on me most miserably . . . and so I gave them warning, and have not yet fixed on a local habitation."

We learn from Charles Dickens the younger that his father, before occupying chambers in Furnival's Inn, had apartments in Buckingham Street, and it is, therefore, not unlikely that he went thither from Cecil Street ; the same authority adds that "if he lived in David Copperfield's rooms—as I have no doubt he did—he must have kept house on the top floor of No. 15 on the east side—the house which displays a tablet commemorating its one-time tenancy by Peter the Great, Czar of all the Russias."* David, in describing his chambers, observes that " they were on the top of the house . . . and consisted of a little half-blind entry where you could see hardly anything, a little stone-blind pantry where you could see nothing at all, a sitting-room, and a bedroom. The furniture was rather faded, but quite good enough for me ; and, sure enough, the river was outside the windows." Here, or at Cecil Street, Dickens doubtless met that martyr to " the spazzums," the immortal Mrs. Crupp, and the " young gal" whom she hired for festive occasions, such as David's dinner-party.

* Another popular novelist, William Black, also lived in this house, and, it is believed, in the selfsame rooms.

In 1832, after gaining experience at Doctors'
Commons, an opening was found for a reporter on
the staff of the *True Sun*, a London morning paper,
then just launched ; and here it may be observed
that newspaper reporting in those days, before railways and electric telegraphs, was not unattended by
great difficulties and even danger, for Dickens himself relates how he had frequently to travel by post-
chaise to remote parts of the country to record
important speeches, and how, on the return journey,
he transcribed his notes on the palm of his hand by
the light of a dark lantern while galloping at fifteen
miles an hour at the dead of night through a wild
district, sometimes finding himself belated in miry
country roads during the small hours in a wheelless
carriage, with exhausted horses and drunken post-
boys, and then succeeding in reaching the office in
time for publication.   While thus representing the
True Sun he joined the reporting staff of the *Mirror
of Parliament* (then a comparatively new paper, conducted by his uncle, John Henry Barrow, barrister-
at-law), and in 1834 associated himself with the
Morning Chronicle,* one of the leading London
journals, and a formidable rival of the *Times*.

As a Parliamentary reporter he won great and
enviable distinction, it being an undoubted fact that
of the eighty or ninety so employed with him in the
" gallery " of the House of Commons, he retained
the premier position by reason of his marvellous
dexterity, accuracy, and capacity for work.   It was,
of course, in the *old* House, not the present palatial

* The office of the *Morning Chronicle* was at No. 332, Strand,
opposite Somerset House, the building having been recently
demolished for improvements in widening the thoroughfare.

1 RAYMOND BUILDINGS, GRAY'S INN. (*Page* 41.)

In the corner house were the offices of Ellis and Blackmore, attorneys, with whom Dickens
was a clerk in 1827-1828.

edifice, that Charles Dickens followed this avocation, where the accommodation provided for the newspaper representatives proved most unsatisfactory, the " gallery " in the House of Lords being no better than a " preposterous pen " (as Dickens described it), in which the reporters were " huddled together like so many sheep," while the reporters in the Commons carried on their duties in the Strangers' Gallery until a separate gallery was provided for their use in the temporary House constructed in 1834. The " gentlemen of the press " are now treated with much greater consideration ; instead of the dark lobby, or " pen," there are large writing - rooms, separate apartments for smoking, reading, dining, and dressing, as well as a stationer's shop, a post-office, and a refreshment-bar.

Dickens's final appearance at the House of Commons as a reporter was at the close of the session of 1836, when, like David Copperfield, he " noted down the music of the Parliamentary bagpipes for the last time." For he had already tasted the delights of authorship, having written some original papers for the *Evening Chronicle* and other periodicals, and henceforth he determined to adopt literature as a profession. His first paper appeared (entitled " A Dinner at Poplar Walk ")* anonymously in the *Monthly Magazine* nearly three years prior to his retirement from the Press Gallery—that is, in December, 1833—and he has himself described how, " with fear and trembling," he stealthily dropped the manuscript into " a dark letter-box, in a dark office, up a dark court in Fleet Street," and how suffused

* Reprinted as " Mr. Minns and his Cousin " in " Sketches by Boz."

with tears of joy and pride were the eyes of the young author when he beheld his little effusion "in all the glory of print" that "they could not bear the street and were not fit to be seen there." The "dark court" referred to was Johnson's Court, Fleet Street, the location of the office of the old (and long since defunct) *Monthly Magazine;* the court still exists, but the office was demolished quite recently for the extension of the premises of Mr. Henry Sells, who, happily, has preserved, as a memorial of the novelist, the door to which the veritable "dark letter-box" was attached. The story of Dickens's early essays has often been related, and needs no repetition here. Suffice it to say that upon the success or failure of that maiden effort a very great deal depended, as he intended to be guided by the dictum of the publisher and of the public, and there is every probability that, had this initial sketch been unfavourably received, the young writer would have directed his attention to the stage, which for him always possessed a magnetic attraction ; thus, instead of becoming a famous author, he would have blossomed into a popular actor, thereby missing his true vocation.

CHAPTER III.

DICKENS's earlier sketches (which bore no signature until August, 1834, when he adopted the pseudonym of " Boz ") were penned when living with his father in Bentinck Street. At first they yielded no honorarium ; but as soon as he received a modest fee for them in addition to his salary as a reporter, he exhibited a sense of independence in resolving to take the apartments in Buckingham Street, whence he presently removed to more commodious chambers in Furnival's Inn, Holborn. He was then twenty-two years of age, and still on the staff of the *Morning Chronicle*, and from Christmas, 1834, he rented a " three-pair back " at No. 13, Furnival's Inn. One of his earliest (undated) letters bears the address of Furnival's Inn, in which he informs his future brother-in-law, Henry Austin, that he is about to start on a journey, alone and in a gig, to Essex and Suffolk——evidently on journalistic business for the *Morning Chronicle*—and expresses a belief that he would be spilt before paying a turnpike, or run over a child before reaching Chelmsford ; his journey covered the same ground as that performed by Mr. Pickwick in his drive by coach to Ipswich. Twelve months

9

later he transferred his impedimenta from No. 13 to more cheerful rooms at No. 15, renting a "three-pair floor south." Several of the later "Sketches by Boz" were doubtless written at No. 13, which stood squeezed into a corner of the square on the right as entered from Holborn, the young author's modest quarters being almost at the top of a steep and dark staircase.

His rooms at No. 15 were a decided improvement on these, and he probably had them in his mind when referring to Furnival's Inn in "Martin Chuzzlewit" and to John Westlock's apartments there, "two stories up": "There are snug chambers in those Inns where the bachelors live, and, for the dissolute fellows they pretend to be, it is quite surprising how well they get on. . . . His rooms were the perfection of neatness and convenience. . . . There is little enough to see in Furnival's Inn. It is a shady, quiet place, echoing to the footsteps of the stragglers who have business there, and rather monotonous and gloomy on Sunday evenings." It does not require much stretch of imagination to believe that the description of Traddles' chambers in Gray's Inn (vide "David Copperfield," chap. lix.) was drawn from these very apartments, or to realize the probability that the reference to Traddles and his lovely girl guests is a reminiscence of Dickens's own.

This humble abode ever remained in his memory as a hallowed spot, cherished by the fact that here he received the commission to write "Pickwick" and penned the opening chapters, by which immortal achievement he suddenly leaped into fame; but also by another interesting and very personal

YORK HOUSE, 15 BUCKINGHAM STREET, STRAND. (*Page* 45.)

Charles Dickens lodged in the house overlooking the river about 1834, and Mrs. Crupps
let apartments here to David Copperfield.   This house was also occupied
by Peter the Great, Henry Fielding, and William Black.

recollection, namely, that it was the scene of his early domestic life. For, be it remembered, the publication of the first number of "Pickwick" (April, 1836) synchronized with his marriage, the lady of his choice being Catherine Thomson Hogarth, eldest daughter of George Hogarth, one of his colleagues on the staff of the *Morning Chronicle*, the ceremony being performed at the Church of St. Luke, Chelsea, of which parish the Rev. Charles Kingsley (father of the author of "Westward Ho!") then officiated as rector.

The honeymoon over, Dickens and his bride returned to London, and made their home at No. 15, Furnival's Inn, where their eldest child, Charles, was born. Here his favourite sister-in-law, Mary Hogarth, sometimes stayed with the youthful couple, her amiable and delightful disposition proving a very joy in the little household; her premature death in 1837, in Doughty Street, at the age of seventeen, so unnerved her admiring brother-in-law that the course of "Pickwick" and "Oliver Twist" (produced almost simultaneously) was temporarily interrupted, and writing presently to Mrs. Hogarth from his next abode, he said: "I wish you could know how I weary now for the three rooms in Furnival's Inn, and how I miss that pleasant smile and those sweet words which, bestowed upon our evening's work, on our merry banterings round the fire, were more precious to me than the applause of a whole world would be." Here, too (as already mentioned), lived John Westlock when visited by Tom Pinch, and it was the scene, also, of certain incidents in "The Mystery of Edwin Drood." Does not Mr. Grewgious (whose chambers were "over the way" at Staple Inn) tell us that

" Furnival's is fireproof and specially watched and lighted," and did he not escort Rosa Bud to her rooms there, at Wood's Hotel in the Square, afterwards confiding her to the care of the " Unlimited head chambermaid "?*

It was once an Inn of Chancery attached to Lincoln's Inn, deriving its name from Sir William Furnivall, who owned much property hereabouts. About 1818 it became a series of chambers wholly unconnected with any Inn of Court, and in that year was entirely rebuilt by Peto. On the right-hand side of the Square, as immediately entered from Holborn, the house (No. 15) containing the bright little rooms once tenanted by Dickens was easily identified in later years by the medallion above the ground-floor windows which notified the fact ; this house and its neighbour were more ornate than the rest, by reason of the series of Ionic pilasters between the windows. The whole of Furnival's Inn was swept away in 1898, and the site covered by an extension of the premises of the Prudential Insurance Company ; thus, alas ! disappears an extremely interesting Dickens landmark, so intimately associated with the novelist and his writings.

Dickens must have relinquished his tenancy of the chambers in Furnival's Inn before the actual term had expired, the assumption being that he had taken them on a short lease, as, according to the official record, he continued to pay rent until February 1839. Two years previously, finding this accom-

* A writer in *Middlesex and Hertfordshire Notes and Queries*, July, 1895, states that Dickens also occupied for some months a suite of rooms in Wood's Hotel (Furnival's Inn) on the first-floor, south-east corner of the main building.

modation inadequate, and realizing that his literary labours had already begun to yield a good income, he determined to take a house, No. 48, Doughty Street, Mecklenburgh Square—a locality not otherwise unknown to literary fame ; for Shirley Brooks (a former editor of *Punch*) was born in this street, while both Sydney Smith and Edmund Yates lived there, the latter at No. 43,* opposite Tegg, the publisher of the " Peter Parley " series of juvenile books.

Yates, in his " Recollections and Experiences," recalls the Doughty Street of his day (and of Dickens's) as " a broad, airy, wholesome street ; none of your common thoroughfares, to be rattled through by vulgar cabs and earth-shaking Pickford vans, but a self-included property, with a gate at each end, and a lodge with a porter in a gold-laced hat and the Doughty arms† on the buttons of his mulberry-coloured coat, to prevent anyone, except with a mission to one of the houses, from intruding on the exclusive territory." The lodges and gates have been removed since this was written, and the porter in official garb disappeared with that exclusiveness and quietude which

---

* The date of Edmund Yates's residence here was 1854 *et seq.* The rent of his house (he says) was £70 a year, "on a repairing lease" (which means an annual outlay of from £25 to £30 to keep the bricks and mortar and timbers together), and the accommodation consisted of a narrow dining-room, a little back bedroom, two big drawing-rooms, two good bedrooms, three attics, with kitchen and cellar in the basement. This description conveys an idea of the character and rental value of Dickens's home, five doors distant.

† The property hereabouts is owned by the Doughty family, and belongs to the notorious Tichborne estate.

doubtless attracted Dickens to the spot more than sixty years ago.

No. 48, Doughty Street (where his daughters Mary and Kate were born) is situated on the east side of the street, and contains twelve rooms—a single-fronted, three-storied house, with a railed-in area in front and a small garden at the rear. A tiny little room on the ground-floor, facing the garden, is believed to have been the novelist's study, in which he wrote the latter portion of " Pickwick," and practically the whole of " Oliver Twist " and " Nicholas Nickleby." The summer months he customarily spent away from home, taking his work with him, and thus a few chapters of these books were penned at Broadstairs, at Twickenham Park, and at Elm Cottage (now called Elm Lodge), Petersham, a pretty little rural retreat rented by him in the summer of 1839, a locality to which he then referred as " those remote and distant parts, with the chain of mountains formed by Richmond Hill presenting an almost insurmountable barrier between me and the busy world."

At Elm Cottage he frequently enjoyed the society of his friends — Maclise, Landseer, Ainsworth, Talfourd, and the rest—many of whom joined in athletic competitions organized by their energetic host in the extensive grounds, among other frivolities being a balloon club for children, of which Forster was elected president on condition that he supplied all the balloons. Elm Cottage (Lodge) is now a school, screened from the public road by a high wooden fence and a barrier of elm-trees ; it is a heavy-looking structure, roofed with red tiles, and at the rear is Sudbrook Lane. The novelist's first

15 FURNIVAL'S INN, HOLBORN. *(Page 50.)*

From a sketch by the late F. G. Kitton. Reproduced by kind permission of
Messrs. T. C. and E. C. Jack.

country home, however, was at No. 4, Ailsa Park Villas, Twickenham, still standing in the Isleworth Road,* near St. Margaret's railway-station, described in a recent issue of the *Richmond and Twickenham Times* as "a building on regular lines, shut in from the world by a plenitude of trees, silent and quiet, an ideal cottage for a mind seeking rest and repose;" not a picturesque edifice by any means, but having a quaint entablature with a circular window in the centre thereof, the house having since undergone little or no change, except, perhaps, in the enlargement of the balcony over the main entrance. There are several references in Dickens's early letters to this region of the Thames Valley (to the Star and Garter, at Richmond, Eel Pie Island, etc.), and much local colouring is employed in certain of his novels— "Nicholas Nickleby," "Little Dorrit," and especially in "Oliver Twist."* It is interesting to know that the Old Coach and Horses at Isleworth, where Sikes and Oliver halted during the burglary expedition to Chertsey, remains almost intact to this day, opposite Syon Lane, and contiguous to Syon House, the residence of that popular writer of fiction, Mr. George Manville Fenn.*

It was during the Doughty Street days that Dickens, in order to relieve the mental tension, indulged in many enjoyable jaunts into the country with Forster, these acting as a stimulant to fresh exertion. He either rode on horseback or walked to such outlying districts as Hampstead, Barnet, or

* I am indebted for many of these particulars to Mr. E. J. Line, author of an illustrated article entitled "The Thames Valley of Charles Dickens," printed in the *Richmond and Twickenham Times*, December 24, 1903.

Richmond, his favourite haunt in the northern suburb being Jack Straw's Castle on the Heath, famous also for its associations with Thackeray, Du Maurier, and Lord Leighton, and commemorated a generation before by Washington Irving in his "Tales of a Traveller." Here the Dickens traditions are still cherished, a small upper apartment in front being pointed out as the bedroom which he occasionally occupied. "I knows a good 'ous there," he said to Forster when imploring his companionship on a bout to Hampstead, "where we can have a red-hot chop for dinner and a glass of wine"; and the notification resulted in many happy meetings there in the coming years.* A writer in the *Daily Graphic* (July 18, 1903) avers that Hampstead possesses other Dickensian associations—that the novelist had lodgings at Wylde's Farm, and, it is said, wrote some chapters of "Bleak House" in the picturesque cottage, which, with the farmhouse and land, it is proposed to acquire for the use and enjoyment of the public. Wylde's Farm is situated on the north-west boundary of Hampstead Heath, close to North End, Hampstead ; it formerly consisted of two farms, one

* "Jack Straw's Castle, also known as the Castle Hotel, which stands on elevated ground near the large pond and the flagstaff, has been somewhat modernized of late years. It has been generally supposed that the name of this hostelry is derived from the well-known peasant leader in the terrible rising of Richard II.'s time; but Professor Hales assures us there is no sufficient authority for the tradition, for the present designation is perhaps not older than the middle of the eighteenth century, the original sign being most likely The Castle, without any preceding genitive, Richardson, for example, thus referring to it in 'Clarissa Harlowe,' 1748. For the connection of Jack Straw with Hampstead there is apparently no historic defence." —*The Home Counties Magazine*, April, 1899.

48 DOUGHTY STREET.   (*Page* 54.)

The residence of Charles Dickens, 1837-1839.   His only London residence which remains
unchanged.   Part of " Pickwick," " Oliver Twist," and the greater
part of " Nickleby " were written here.

known as Collins's and the other as Tooley's, and it was at Collins's that John Linnell, the artist, lived for some years, and there welcomed, as visitors, William Blake, Mulready, Flaxman, George Morland, and others distinguished in Art and Literature.

The associations of the novelist with No. 48, Doughty Street are perpetuated not only in the name "Dickens House" recently bestowed upon it, but by the tablet affixed thereon by the London County Council in December last—truly, a long-delayed tribute, and especially deserving in this case owing to the fact that it is the only London home of Charles Dickens which survives intact structurally. It was here that in September, 1838, Forster lunched with him, and then to sit, read, or work, "or do something" (as the author expressed it in his note of invitation), "while I write the *last* chapter of 'Oliver,' which will be arter a lamb chop." "How well I remember that evening!" observes his friend, "and our talk of what should be the fate of Charley Bates, on behalf of whom (as, indeed, for the Dodger, too) Talfourd* had pleaded as earnestly in mitigation of judgment as ever at the bar for any client he had most respected."

Writing to his friend Macready, the actor, in November, 1839, Dickens said : "You must come and see my new house when we have it to rights." He had just completed the last number of "Nicholas Nickleby," when he decided to leave Doughty Street for a more commodious residence in a more exclusive

* Serjeant (afterwards Justice) Talfourd, to whom "Pickwick" was dedicated. He composed a sonnet "To Charles Dickens, on his 'Oliver Twist,'" and declared that this story was the most delightful he had ever read.

neighbourhood, namely, No. 1, Devonshire Terrace, York Gate—"a house of great promise (and great premium), undeniable situation, and excessive splendour," to quote his own concise description ; it had a large garden, and was shut out from the New Road (now the Marylebone Road) by a high brick wall facing the York Gate into Regent's Park. In "The Uncommercial Traveller," Dickens refers to "having taken the lease of a house in a certain distinguished Metropolitan parish—a house which then appeared to me to be a frightfully first-class Family Mansion, involving awful responsibilities."*

A contemporary drawing of the house by Daniel Maclise, R.A., represents it as detached and standing in its own grounds, with a wrought-iron entrance-gate surmounted by a lamp-bracket ; the building consisted of a basement, two stories, and an attic. There are only three houses in the Terrace, and immediately beyond is the burial-ground of St. Marylebone Church.† No. 1, Devonshire Terrace is now semi-detached, having a line of taller residential structures on the southern side, while a portion of the high brick wall on the Terrace side has been replaced by an iron railing. The house

* "Some Recollections of Mortality," first printed in *All the Year Round*, May 16, 1863.

† This church figures prominently in Hogarth's paintings of "The Rake's Progress." It was the scene also of Byron's baptism and of the marriage of the Brownings.

Apropos, it may be mentioned that in 1843, during Dickens's residence in the parish of St. Marylebone, he took sittings for a year or two in the Little Portland Street Unitarian Chapel, for whose officiating minister, Edward Tagart, he had a warm regard, which continued long after he had ceased to be a member of the congregation.

JACK-STRAW'S CASTLE, HAMPSTEAD, CIRCA 1835. (*Page* 56.)

From a print in the collection of Councillor Newton, Hampstead.

itself has been structurally changed since Dickens's days, and has undergone enlargement, a new story being inserted between the ground-floor and the upper story, thus considerably altering its original proportions without actually removing its principal features. Mr. Hughes, who in 1888 examined the house prior to these "improvements," states that it then contained thirteen rooms. "The polished mahogany doors in the hall, and the chaste Italian marble mantelpieces in the principal rooms, are said to have been put up by the novelist. On the ground-floor the smaller room to the east-ward of the house, with windows facing north and looking into the pleasant garden, where the plane-trees and turf are beautifully green, is pointed out as having been his study."* Concerning Dickens's studies, his eldest daughter tells us that they " were always cheery, pleasant rooms, and always, like him-self, the personification of neatness and tidiness. On the shelf of his writing-table were many dainty and useful ornaments—gifts from his friends or members of his family—and always a vase of bright and fresh flowers." Referring to the sanctum at Devonshire Terrace, Miss Dickens observes that it (the first she could remember) was "a pretty room, with steps leading directly into the garden from it, and with an extra baize door to keep out all sounds and noise." The garden here constituted a great attraction to Dickens, for it enabled him, with his children and friends, to indulge in such simple games as battle-dore and shuttlecock and bowls, which not only delighted him, but conveniently afforded means of

* "A Week's Tramp in Dickens Land," by W. R. Hughes, 1891.

obtaining necessary exercise and recreation at intervals during his literary labours.

In a stable on the south side of the garden were kept the two ravens that inspired the conception of Grip in " Barnaby Rudge," of which famous bird they were the " great originals." Longfellow, after visiting the novelist here in 1841, said in a letter to a friend : " I write this from Dickens's study, the focus from which so many luminous things have radiated. The raven croaks in the garden, and the ceaseless roar of London fills my ears." The first raven died in 1841 from the effects (it was believed) of a meal of white paint ; he was quickly succeeded by an older and a larger raven (" comparatively of weak intellect "), whose decease in 1845 was similarly premature, probably owing to " the same illicit taste for putty and paint which had been fatal to his predecessor." " Voracity killed him," said Dickens, " as it did Scott's ; he died unexpectedly by the kitchen fire. He kept his eye to the last upon the meat as it roasted, and suddenly turned over on his back with a sepulchral cry of ' Cuckoo.' " The novelist occupied No. 1, Devonshire Terrace (the scene of many of his literary triumphs) for a period of about twelve years—the happiest period of his life—and there wrote some of the best of his stories, including " The Old Curiosity Shop," " Barnaby Rudge," " Martin Chuzzlewit," " Dombey and Son," and " David Copperfield," the latter the most delightful of all his books, and his own favourite. Here also he composed those ever-popular Yule-tide annuals, " A Christmas Carol," " The Cricket on the Hearth," and " The Haunted Man."

The friends which the fame of the young author

attracted thither included some of the most distinguished men of the day, such as Macready, Talfourd, Proctor ("Barry Cornwall"), Clarkson Stanfield, R.A., Sir David Wilkie, R.A., Sir Edwin Landseer, R.A., Samuel Rogers, Sydney Smith, and many others of equal note, for which reason, among others, he always cherished fond recollections of this London home, and writing to Forster from Genoa in 1844, he could not refrain from expressing how strangely he felt in the midst of such unfamiliar environment. "I seem," he said, "as if I had plucked myself out of my proper soil when I left Devonshire Terrace, and would take root no more until I return to it. . . . Did I tell you how many fountains we have here? No matter.   If they played nectar they wouldn't please me half so well as the West Middlesex Waterworks at Devonshire Terrace."   As in the case of 48, Doughty Street, this house bears a commemorative tablet, placed by the London County Council. It is interesting to add that within a stone's-throw stands the old parish church of St. Marylebone, the scene of the burial of little Paul Dombey and his mother, and of Mr. Dombey's second marriage.

At Devonshire Terrace four sons were born to him, viz., Walter Landor, Francis Jeffrey, Alfred Tennyson, Henry Fielding, and one daughter, Dora Annie, who survived only a few months.

On particular occasions, owing to a prolonged absence from England, he let this house firstly to General Sir John Wilson in 1842 (when he first visited America); secondly, to a widow lady, who agreed to occupy it during his stay in Italy in 1844;

and, thirdly, in 1846, to Sir James Duke. The widow lady took possession a week or two before he started for the Continent, thus compelling him to seek temporary quarters elsewhere. He found the necessary accommodation near at hand, namely, at No. 9, Osnaburgh Terrace, New Road (now Euston Road), which he rented for the interval. Here occurred an amusing contretemps. Before entering upon this brief tenancy, he had invited a number of valued friends to a farewell dinner prior to his departure for Italy, and suddenly discovered that, owing to the small dimensions of the rooms, he would be obliged to abandon or postpone the function, the house having no convenience " for the production of any other banquet than a cold collation of plate and linen, the only comforts we have not left behind us." Additional help being obtained, however, the dinner went off satisfactorily.

Dickens and his family left England for Italy in July, 1844, remaining abroad for a period of twelve months. In November, however, he made a quick journey to London, in order to test the effect of a reading aloud of his just completed Christmas book, " The Chimes," before a few friends assembled for that purpose at Forster's residence, Lincoln's Inn Fields, which, as readers of " Bleak House " may remember, is introduced into that story as Mr. Tulkinghorn's Chambers. The pleasurable interlude over, the novelist returned to Genoa, there remaining until June, 1845, when, homesick and eager to renew the "happy old walks and old talks" with his friends in the " dear old home," he gladly settled down again in Devonshire Terrace. But only eleven months

I DEVONSHIRE TERRACE. (*Page* 58.)

The residence of Dickens, 1839-1851. Some of his finest books were written here.

elapsed before he departed for Switzerland, where he rented a little villa called Rosemont at Lausanne; here he embarked upon a new story, " Dombey and Son," and wrote " The Battle of Life." His stay on the Continent was unexpectedly curtailed by the illness from scarlet fever of his eldest son Charles, then at King's College school in London, whereupon, at the end of February, 1847, the novelist and his wife hastily made their way to the bedside of their sick boy, taking up their abode at the Victoria Hotel, Euston Square,* the Devonshire Terrace home being still occupied by Sir James Duke. The little invalid was under the care of his grandmother, Mrs. Hogarth, in Albany Street, Regent's Park, and Dickens secured temporary quarters near at hand, in Chester Place, where he remained until June, and where a fifth son was born, christened Sydney Smith Haldemand.

Writing to Mrs. Hogarth from Chester Place (the number is not recorded), he said: " This house is very cheerful on the drawing-room floor and above, looking into the park on one side and Albany Street on the other."

Early in 1848 Devonshire Terrace was quitted by Sir James Duke, and Dickens returned to London from Brighton (where he had been spending two or three weeks) joyfully to enter into possession once more of his own home, taking with him for completion an important chapter of " Dombey and Son." The lease of this house expired in 1851, the last book written there being " David Copperfield," at

* The Euston and Victoria Hotel no longer exists. It stood in Euston Grove, at No. 14, Euston Square (north side).

the publication of which his reputation attained its highest level. He now realized that, for a family consisting of six sons and two daughters (of whom the eldest, Charles Culliford Boz, was but fourteen years of age), this residence did not offer sufficient accommodation, and therefore he decided with keen regret not to renew the lease.* Indeed, from the beginning of the year he had been negotiating for a more commodious domicile, Tavistock House, in Tavistock Square, then, and for some years previously, the residence of his cherished artist friend, Frank Stone, A.R.A., father of Mr. Marcus Stone, the Royal Academician. An opportunity arising for the immediate purchase of the lease of Tavistock House, Dickens felt convinced it was prudent that he should buy it, for, as he observed in a letter to Frank Stone, it seemed very unlikely that he would obtain " the same comforts for the rising generation elsewhere for the same money," and gave him carte-blanche to make the necessary arrangements for acquiring the lease at a price not exceeding £1,500. " I don't make any apologies," he added, " for thrusting this honour upon you, knowing what a thorough-going old pump you are." After securing the property, the summer months were spent by the novelist at Broadstairs, where a " dim vision " suddenly confronted him in connection with the impending change of residence. " Supposing," he wrote considerately to Stone, " you should find, on looking forward, a probability of your being houseless at Michaelmas, what do you say to using Devonshire

* No. 1, Devonshire Terrace was at one time the home of George du Maurier, the well-known *Punch* artist. It is now partly utilized as solicitors' offices.

9 OSNABURGH TERRACE. *(Page 62.)*

Occupied by Dickens in the summer of 1844.

Terrace as a temporary encampment? It will not be in its usual order, but we would take care that there should be as much useful furniture of all sorts there as to render it unnecessary for you to move a stick. If you should think this a convenience, then I should propose to you to pile your furniture in the middle of the rooms at Tavistock House, and go out to Devonshire Terrace two or three weeks *before* Michaelmas, to enable my workmen to commence their operations. This might be to our mutual convenience, and therefore I suggest it. Certainly, the sooner I can begin on Tavistock House the better, and possibly your going into Devonshire Terrace might relieve you from a difficulty that would otherwise be perplexing. I make this suggestion (I need not say to *you*) solely on the chance of its being useful to both of us. If it were merely convenient to me, you know I shouldn't dream of it. Such an arrangement, while it would cost you nothing, would perhaps enable you to get your new house into order comfortably, and do exactly the same thing for me."* The exchange was accordingly made, so enabling Dickens to effect certain structural improvements in Tavistock House before returning from Broadstairs to take possession in November. These alterations and reparations, which were apparently on a somewhat extensive scale, were carried out under the superintendence of his brother-in-law, Henry Austin, an architect and sanitary engineer, to whom Dickens (harassed by delays in the work) wrote despairingly as follows:

* The artist removed to another residence in the Square, not more than a couple of houses from that of Dickens.

" Broadstairs,
" *Sunday, September* 7, 1851.

" My dear Henry,

   " I am in that state of mind which you may
(once) have seen described in the newspapers as
' bordering on distraction,' the house given up to
me, the fine weather going on (soon to break, I dare
say), the printing season oozing away, my new book
(' Bleak House ') waiting to be born, and

" *No Workmen on the Premises,*

along of my not hearing from you ! !   I have torn
all my hair off, and constantly beat my unoffending
family.   Wild notions have occurred to me of sending
in my own plumber to do the drains.   Then I remember that you have probably written to propose
your man, and restrain my audacious hand.   Then
Stone presents himself, with a most exasperatingly
mysterious visage, and says that a rat has appeared
in the kitchen, and it's his opinion (Stone's, not the
rat's) that the drains want ' compo-ing '; for the use
of which explicit language I could fell him without
remorse.   In my horrible desire to ' compo ' everything, the very postman becomes my enemy, because
he brings no letter from you ; and, in short, I don't
see what's to become of me unless I hear from you
to-morrow, which I have not the least expectation of
doing.

   " Going over the house again, I have materially
altered the plans, abandoned conservatory and front
balcony, decided to make Stone's painting-room the
drawing-room (it is nearly 6 inches higher than the
room below), to carry the entrance passage right
through the house to a back door leading to the

garden, and to reduce the once intended drawing-room — now schoolroom — to a manageable size, making a door of communication between the new drawing-room and the study. Curtains and carpets, on a scale of awful splendour and magnitude, are already in preparation, and still—still—

"*No Workmen on the Premises.*

"To pursue this theme is madness. Where are you? When are you coming home? Where is *the* man who is to do the work? Does he know that an army of artificers must be turned in at once, and the whole thing finished out of hand?

"O rescue me from my present condition. Come up to the scratch, I entreat and implore you!

"I send this to Lætitia (Mrs. Austin) to forward,

"Being, as you well know why,
   Completely floored by N.W.,* I
     Sleep!

I hope you may be able to read this. My state of mind does not admit of coherence.

"Ever affectionately,
"CHARLES DICKENS.

"P.S.—*No Workmen* on the *Premises!*
"Ha! ha! ha! (I am laughing demoniacally.)"†

Other letters followed, testifying to the highly nervous condition and impatience of the writer, who in certain of these characteristic missives, said:

* *I.e.*, no workmen.
† First printed in "The Letters of Charles Dickens."

"I am perpetually wandering (in fancy) up and down the house (Tavistock House) and tumbling over the workmen ; when I feel that they are gone to dinner, I become low ; when I look forward to their total abstinence on Sundays, I am wretched. The gravy at dinner has a taste of glue in it. I smell paint in the sea. Phantom lime attends me all the day long. I dream that I am a carpenter, and can't partition off the hall. I frequently dance (with a distinguished company) in the dressing-room, and fall in the kitchen for want of a pillar. . . . I dream, also, of the workmen every night. They make faces at me, and won't do anything. . . Oh ! if this were to last long ; the distractions of the new book, the whirling of the story through one's mind, escorted by workmen, the imbecility, the wild necessity of beginning to write, the not being able to do so, the — O ! I should go——O !"*

The house, after all, was not ready to receive him at the stipulated time, for it proved to be as difficult to get the workmen off the premises as to get them on, and at the end of October they were still busy in their own peculiar manner, the painters mislaying their brushes every five minutes, and chiefly whistling in the intervals, while the carpenters " continued to look sideways with one eye down pieces of wood, as if they were absorbed in the contemplation of the perspective of the Thames Tunnel, and had entirely relinquished the vanities of this transitory world." With white lime in the kitchens, blank paper constantly spread on drawing-room walls and shred off again, men clinking at the new stair-rails, Irish

* First printed in " The Letters of Charles Dickens."

labourers howling in the schoolroom ("but I don't know why"), the gardener vigorously lopping the trees, something like pandemonium reigned supreme, and the "Inimitable" mentally blessed the day when silence and order at length succeeded, permitting him once more to settle down to his desk, and to concentrate his thoughts upon the new serial, "Bleak House," the writing of which was begun at the end of November, 1851—on a Friday, too, regarded by him as his lucky day.

Tavistock House,* with Russell House and Bedford House adjoining (all the property of the Duke of Bedford and all demolished), stood at the northeast corner of the private, secluded Tavistock Square (named after the Marquis of Tavistock, father of the celebrated William, Lord Russell), a short distance south of Euston Road, about midway between Euston Square and the aristocratic Russell Square, and railed off from Upper Woburn Place.

The exterior of Tavistock House (pulled down

---

* Tavistock House was for many years the residence of James Perry (editor of Dickens's old paper, the *Morning Chronicle*, in its best days), and was then noted for its reunions of men of political and literary distinction. Eliza Cook, the poetess, also lived in Tavistock House when she left Greenhithe, Kent, and Mary Russell Mitford (authoress of "Our Village") became an honoured guest there in 1818. The house was afterwards divided, and the moiety, which still retained the name of Tavistock, became the home of Frank Stone.

From the front windows of Tavistock House, which stood immediately on the right on entering the railed-in garden or square, the spire of St. Pancras Church was plainly visible, being but a short distance away. The pillars of the gateway leading to the enclosure were (and are) surmounted by quaint lamps with iron supports. Dickens held the lease from the Duke of Bedford at a "peppercorn" ground-rent.

in 1901) presented a plain brick structure of two stories in height above the ground-floor, with attics in the roof, an open portico or porch being added by a later tenant ; it contained no less than eighteen rooms, including a drawing-room capable of holding more than three hundred persons. On the garden side, at the rear, the house had a bowed front somewhat resembling that at Devonshire Terrace. Hans Christian Andersen, who visited him here in 1857, has left us a delightful record of his impressions of the mansion :

"In Tavistock Square stands Tavistock House. This and the strip of garden in front are shut out from the thoroughfare (Gordon Place, on the east side) by an iron railing. A large garden, with a grass plot and high trees, stretches behind the house, and gives it a countrified look in the midst of this coal and gas - steaming London. In the passage from street to garden hung pictures and engravings. Here stood a marble bust of Dickens, so like him, so youthful and handsome ; and over a bedroom door were inserted the bas-reliefs of Night and Day, after Thorwaldsen.* On the first floor was a rich library, with a fireplace and a writing-table, looking out on the garden. . . . The kitchen was underground, and at the top of the house were bedrooms. I had a snug room looking out on the garden, and over

* The portrait-bust was probably that executed in marble by Dickens's beloved friend Angus Fletcher ("Poor Kindheart," as the novelist called him), whose mother was an English beauty and heiress. He died in 1862. At the sale of Dickens's effects in 1870, the bust realized fifty-one guineas, and it would be interesting to know its present destination. The pair of reliefs after Thorwaldsen were disposed of on the same occasion for eight and a half guineas.

the tree-tops I saw the London towers and spires appear and disappear as the weather cleared or thickened."

Dickens's eldest daughter, in recalling her father's study at Tavistock House, remembered it as being larger and more ornate than his previous sanctum, and describes it as "a fine large room, opening into the drawing-room by means of sliding doors. When the rooms were thrown together," she adds, "they gave my father a promenade of considerable length for the constant indoor walking which formed a favourite recreation for him after a hard day's writing." Here were wholly or partly written some of his best stories—viz., "Bleak House," "Hard Times," "Little Dorrit," "A Tale of Two Cities," and "Great Expectations," his labours being agreeably diversified by private theatricals.

With a view to possibilities of this kind, he caused the school-room (on the ground-floor at the back of the house) to be adapted for such entertainments by having a stage erected and a platform built outside the window for scenic purposes. His older children (the last of the family, Edward Bulwer Lytton, was born in Tavistock House, 1852) had now attained an age that justified a demand for a special form of home amusement, and this met with a ready response from an indulgent father, who, mainly, if not entirely, for their delight, arranged for a series of juvenile theatricals, which began on the first Twelfth Night there (the eldest son's fifteenth birthday) with a performance of Fielding's burlesque, "Tom Thumb," with Mark Lemon and Dickens himself in the cast. Thackeray, who was present, thoroughly enjoyed the fun, rolling off his seat in a burst of laughter at the absurdity of the thing. Play-bills were printed, and every detail carried out in the orthodox style, for Dickens (who, as " Lessee and Manager," humorously styled himself " Mr. Crummles ") entered heart and soul into the business, and as thoroughly as if his income solely depended on it—this was entirely characteristic of the man.

For the time being, the house was given up to theatrical preparations ; the schoolroom became a painter's shop ; there was a gasfitter's shop all over the basement ; the topmost rooms were devoted to dressmaking, and the novelist's dressing-room to tailoring, while he himself at intervals did his best to write " Little Dorrit " in corners, " like the Sultan's groom, who was turned upside-down by the genii."

The most remarkable performances at " The Smallest Theatre in the World "! (for so the play-bills described it) were the presentations of " The Lighthouse " and " The Frozen Deep," plays specially written by Wilkie Collins, for which the scenes were painted by Clarkson Stanfield, R.A., one of these beautiful works of art (depicting the Eddystone Lighthouse) realizing a thousand guineas after the novelist's death ! These theatrical enter-tainments, continued on Twelfth Nights for many years, were witnessed and enjoyed by many notabili-ties of London (Carlyle among them), and created quite a public sensation.

Dickens's cherished friend, the late Miss Mary Boyle, had vivid and pleasing recollections of Tavistock House and the master spirit who pre--sided over it.

" The very sound of the name," she says, " is

TAVISTOCK HOUSE. (*Page 70.*)

The residence of Dickens, 1851-1860.

From a photograph by Catherine Weed Barnes Ward.

replete to me with memories of innumerable evenings passed in the most congenial and delightful intercourse—dinners where the guests vied with each other in brilliant conversation, whether intellectual, witty, or sparkling ; evenings devoted to music or theatricals. First and foremost of that magic circle was the host himself, always 'one of us,' who invariably drew out what was best and most characteristic in others. . . . I can never forget one evening, shortly after the arrival at Tavistock House, when we danced in the New Year. It seemed like a page cut out of the 'Christmas Carol,' as far, at least, as fun and frolic went."*

It was while living at Tavistock House that Dickens devised the series of imitation book-backs with incongruous titles which were to serve as a decorative feature in his study, and were afterwards transferred, together with Clarkson Stanfield's scenery, to his next home. Here, too, he gave sittings for his portrait to E. M. Ward, R.A., in 1854, in which is seen the strongly-contrasting tints of curtains, carpet, and other accessories, indicating the great writer's passion for colour. The background and other details in the portrait by Mr. W. P. Frith, R.A., in 1859, were also painted in Dickens's study at Tavistock House while he was at work. It has been suggested that the novelist probably found this residence a little too convenient for friends and other callers, whose unexpected visits somewhat interrupted him, and that this may have been a reason for his exodus into the country.

In 1855 the novelist ascertained that a picturesque house at Gad's Hill, near Rochester, the possession

* "Mary Boyle—Her Book," 1901.

of which he declared to be a dream of his childhood, was to be sold, and he at once determined to buy it if possible. In this he succeeded, but it was not until 1860 that he finally left his London abode to make his home at his "little Kentish freehold." During part of the interval he divided his favours between Tavistock House and Gad's Hill Place, usually spending the summer months at his country retreat, furnished merely as a temporary summer residence until September, 1860, when he disposed of the remainder of the lease of the London house to Mr. Davis, a Jewish gentleman. Concerning the transaction, he wrote (on the 4th of the month) to his henchman, W. H. Wills: "Tavistock House is cleared to-day, and possession delivered up. I must say that in all things the purchaser has behaved thoroughly well, and that I cannot call to mind any occasion when I have had money dealings with a Christian that have been so satisfactory, considerate, and trusting." His occupation of Tavistock House covered a period of exactly ten years.

In 1885 and subsequently Tavistock House was occupied as a Jewish College, and it is worthy of note that prior to that date it was tenanted by Gounod, the composer, and by Mrs. Georgina Weldon, the well-known lady litigant, who in 1880 privately issued an extraordinary pamphlet entitled "The Ghastly Consequences of Living in Charles Dickens's House," where she dilates upon an attempt made to forcibly convey her to a lunatic asylum.*

* I quote the opening lines of this eccentric effusion :
"'Great men,' no doubt, have a great deal to answer for. No one will deny that. Their 'genius,' which brings them to

5 HYDE PARK PLACE (NOW 5 MARBLE ARCH). (*Page* 77.)

The centre house, without a porch, was the residence of Dickens in the early part of 1870.

Tavistock House, with its neighbours Bedford
House and Russell House, were razed to the ground

---

the front, and which causes men, women, and children to worship
them for the pleasure their beautiful gifts procure to eyes, ears,
and senses, brings them all much responsibility.

"But who would ever have imagined that their dwellings
may bring grave responsibility and grave trouble to those who
take up their abode in a house which the presence of their
genius has hallowed? I live in Tavistock House, Tavistock
Square, London—a dear house, in a nice, quiet, shady garden,
where grow fine large old plantains (out of the Square proper),
and where in summer, from every window of the house, you
may imagine yourself in the country—the real country! That
sounds very grand and luxurious in London; and though the
mere fact of living in the house has very nearly brought upon
me the most terrible fate which can befall a human being
nowadays—namely, *that of a sane person shut up in a lunatic
asylum, put there for the purpose of being slowly or 'accidentally'
murdered*—I cling to the spot because I have spent the happiest,
the most interesting, and the most illumined part of my life
there; also days of the most bitter anguish, the most heart-
crushing despair, when I was obliged to leave the dear home
and husband for some time, because I could not stop crying.
The thought of my loss and the shipwreck of my life was too
vivid, too much for me. I went away and returned when I had
got calm enough to restrain my tears, but with the sun set for
ever on what remained to me of the summer of middle life. I
love the dear home, too, because my darling puggies are buried
in the garden under the mulberry-tree, without a tombstone,
alas! because ever since they died I have been planning to have
a pretty monument made to mark the spot where they lay, and
that when I have thought I could afford myself that pleasure
somebody has generally stolen my money . . . and I have to
put off ordering the intended *work of art*, which I mean it to
be, till I feel 'flush' again. I was a slave to my dear Dan for
nearly thirteen years, and I think I must have loved that dog as
much as anybody ever loved anything in this world.

"I must not let you wonder too long what I am driving at,
my readers, by telling you that, through the mere fact of living

about four years ago, and the land, to be let on a
building lease, is still a desolate waste.

Although definitely settled at Gad's Hill, Dickens
decided upon taking a furnished house in town for
a few months of the London season for the sake of
his daughters, then young ladies just emerged from
their teens, and the younger of whom was then
engaged to be married. Accordingly, in the spring
months of 1861 we find him and his household
established at No. 3, Hanover Terrace, Regent's
Park, a retired spot adjoining the western side of
the Park. In February, 1862, he made an exchange
of houses for three months with his friends Mr. and
Mrs. Hogge, they going to Gad's Hill, and he and
his family to Mr. Hogge's house at No. 16, Hyde
Park Gate, South Kensington Gore (south side of
Kensington High Street); for, as the novelist ex-

---

in what had been a house where a great man had lived, I nearly
got locked up in a lunatic asylum. You must think me insane,
I fancy, to say such a thing, and I must confess that you might
guess every mortal and immortal thing under the sun, but you
would never guess how this most frightful occurrence took
place.

"Those who have read Charles Dickens's 'Life,' by Mr.
Forster, will know that he is the 'great man' who had lived at
Tavistock House for twelve [ten] years. People from all parts
of the world have come to look at the house Charles Dickens
lived in, and see the interior of the house, a request which I
have frequently complied with."

On another page Mrs. Weldon says: "Although three
keepers got into Tavistock House and actually laid hold of me,
I escaped their delicate intentions, as I consider, by a merciful
interposition of Providence. . . ."

At the Dickens Birthday Celebration, the dancers were
attired in the costumes of Dickens characters, and Mrs. Weldon
appeared in wig and gown—a very fascinating Serjeant
Buzfuz.

plained, his unmarried daughter naturally liked to be in town at that time of the year. In the middle of February, 1864, he removed to another London mansion, No. 57, Gloucester Place, north of Hyde Park, where he stayed until June, busily engaged during those months with "Our Mutual Friend." Gloucester Place now forms part of Gloucester Terrace, near Bayswater Road, and the northern end of the Serpentine.

For the spring of 1865 a furnished house was taken at No. 16, Somers Place, north of Hyde Park (between Cambridge Square and Southwick Crescent), which Dickens, with his sister-in-law and daughter, occupied from the beginning of March until June, while Gad's Hill Place was being "gorgeously painted," as he informed Macready, with a further intimation that, owing to great suffering in his foot, he was a terror to the household, likewise to all the organs and brass bands in this quarter. In 1866 he rented for the spring a furnished house at No. 6, Southwick Place, Hyde Park Square (contiguous to his former residence in Somers Place), and early in January, 1870 (five months before his death), he took for the season the classic-fronted mansion of his friends Mr. and Mrs. Milner-Gibson, at No. 5, Hyde Park Place, apropos of which he said in a letter to his American friend James T. Fields : " We live here (opposite the Marble Arch) in a charming house until the 1st of June, and then return to Gad's. . . . I have a large room here, with three fine windows, overlooking the Park, unsurpassable for airiness and cheerfulness."

This house was Charles Dickens's last London

residence ; he rented it, Forster tells us, for the period of his London Readings at that time, in order to avoid the daily railway journey to London from Gad's Hill, entertaining an especial dislike to that mode of travelling in the then serious state of his health.

At Hyde Park Place he wrote a considerable portion of the unfinished fragment of " The Mystery of Edwin Drood," and made the acquaintance, through his friend Sir John Millais, of the illustrator of that story, Mr. Luke Fildes, now the well-known Royal Academician, who cherishes the most pleasant recollections of the collaboration.

We learn that in 1867 and 1869 Dickens did not take a house in London, as was customary in these later years. In May of 1869 he stayed with his daughter and sister-in-law for two or three weeks at the St. James's Hotel (now the Berkeley), at the corner of Berkeley Street, Piccadilly, having promised to be in London at the time of the arrival of a number of American friends ; in order, too, that he might be near his London doctor for a while,* and be able to avail himself of invitations from innumerable familiar acquaintances.

In 1867, having a series of Readings in town and country alternately, he decided to dispense with unnecessary travelling between Gad's Hill and London by sleeping in bachelor quarters at the office of his weekly journal, *All the Year Round*, which succeeded the earlier publication, *Household Words*, in 1859.

* The neuralgic pain in his foot, originating, he believed, in a prolonged walk in the snow, continued to cause acute suffering, and completely prostrated him at intervals

THE OFFICE OF "ALL THE YEAR ROUND,"
26 (FORMERLY 11) WELLINGTON STREET, STRAND. (*Page* 78.)

In 1860 Dickens furnished rooms here, which were " Really a success   As comfortable, cheerful, and private as anything of the kind can possibly be " (letter to Miss Mamie Dickens).

The office of *All the Year Round* was then No. 11, Wellington Street, North Strand, and still exists as No. 26, Wellington Street, at the south corner of Tavistock Street, at its junction with Wellington Street. In 1872 the lessee of the property was unavailingly approached by emissaries from Chicago with the view of purchasing and transporting the building to the *World's Fair*, as a memento of the novelist. For his own convenience Dickens furnished rooms here,* to be used as bedroom and sitting-room as occasion required, which must have reminded him of those early days when he lived in similar bachelor apartments at Furnival's Inn. Happily for him, his creature comforts were ensured by an old and tried servant—a paragon—whom Dickens declared to be " the cleverest man of his kind in the world," and able to do anything, " from excellent carpentry to excellent cooking."

The office of *Household Words* was situated in Wellington Street, Strand, nearly opposite the portico of the Lyceum Theatre, a short distance from the Strand on the right-hand side of the way, and was rendered somewhat conspicuous by a large bow window. This building stood on the site of a very old tenement, with which there was bound up a very weird London legend, setting forth how the room on the first-floor front was the identical apartment which had served Hogarth as the scene of the final tableau in " The Harlot's Progress." The novelist used to tell his contributors that he had often, while sitting in his editorial sanctum, conjured up mental

---

* At Sotheby's, on December 4, 1902, were sold the office table, two chairs, and a looking-glass, which for many years were in daily requisition by Dickens at the office of *All the Year Round*.

pictures of Kate Hackabout lying dead in her coffin, wept over by drunken beldames.

On September 17, 1903, the London County Council's housebreakers took possession of the old office of *Household Words* (whence in 1850 Dickens launched the first number of that periodical), and the building has since been sacrificed in the general scheme for providing a new thoroughfare from the Strand to Holborn. Dickens used the front-room on the first floor—that with a large bow window— as his editorial sanctum, and on busy nights he slept on the premises instead of returning to Gad's Hill. Latterly this room was used as an office by the manager of the Gaiety Theatre. The projection of the new Kingsway and Aldwych has resulted in the inevitable evanishment of many Dickensian landmarks, for a glance at the plans of these thoroughfares now in course of construction shows that they will cover an important section of "Dickens's London," such as Clare Market, the New Inn, Portugal Street, Drury Lane, Sardinia Street, Kingsgate Street, etc.

*   *   *   *   *

A brief mention of certain public and private institutions in London having more or less informal associations with Dickens will form a fitting conclusion to the present chapter.

In 1838 the author of "Pickwick" (then lately completed) was elected a member of the Athenæum Club, his sponsor being Mr. Serjeant Storks, and continued his membership of that very exclusive confraternity for the rest of his life. The late Rev. F. G. Waugh, author of a booklet on the Athenæum Club, did not think that Dickens considered himself

THE OFFICE OF "HOUSEHOLD WORDS," WELLINGTON STREET, STRAND. (*Page 80.*)

The principal entrance was where the centre window on the ground floor is shown.
The building is now demolished.

a popular member, probably because he seldom spoke to anyone unless previously addressed. When not taking his sandwich standing, his usual seat in the coffee-room was the table on the east side of the room, just south of the fireplace. " I believe," says Mr. Waugh, in a letter to the present writer, "the last letter he wrote from here was to his son, who did not receive it till after his father's death." The club, which preserves the novelist's favourite chair, was the scene, too, of a happy incident—the reconciliation of Thackeray and Dickens after a period of strained relationship. This occurred only a few days before the death of the author of " Vanity Fair," when the two great writers, meeting by accident in the lobby of the club, suddenly turned and saw each other, " and the unrestrained impulse of both was to hold out the hand of forgiveness and fellowship."

> " . . . In the hall, that trysting-place,
> Two severed friends meet face to face :
> 'Tis Boz and Makepeace, good and true
> (' Behind the coats,' hats not a few).
> A start, and both uncertain stand ;
> Then each has clasped the other's hand !"*

The Temple, practically unchanged since Dickens's day, ever remained a favourite locality with him. When quite a young man, and popularly known as " Boz," he entered his name among the students of the Inn of the Middle Temple, though he did not eat dinners there until many years later, and was never called to the Bar. The *Daily News* offices (the old building, not the existing ornate structure) in

* Mr. Percy Fitzgerald, in the *St. James's Gazette*, March 6, 1899.

Bouverie Street are remembered chiefly by the fact that this Liberal newspaper was founded by Dickens, its first editor, in 1846, and a bust-portrait of him may be seen in a niche in the façade of the new building. John Forster's residence, No. 58, Lincoln's Inn Fields, is specially memorable on account of the novelist's associations therewith. Here he was ever a welcome guest, and here, in 1844, he read " The Chimes " from the newly-completed manuscript to an assembled group of friends, the germ of those public readings to which he subsequently devoted so much time and energy. The two houses, Nos. 57 and 58, Lincoln's Inn Fields, were once the town mansion of the Earl of Lindsey. Dickens made Forster's residence the home of Tulkinghorn, the old family lawyer in "Bleak House," whose room with the painted ceiling depicting " fore-shortened allegory " faces the large forecourt, and is now in the occupation of a solicitor ; the painting, however, was obliterated some years ago.

CHAPTER IV.

DICKENS first made acquaintance with many provincial towns during his early newspaper days, when, as a reporter, he galloped by road in post-chaises, both by day and night, to remote parts of the country, meeting with strange adventures, sometimes experiencing awkward predicaments, from which he invariably succeeded in extricating himself and in reaching his destination in good time for publication, his carefully-prepared notes being transcribed, not infrequently, during " the smallest hours of the night in a swift-flying carriage and pair," by the light of a blazing wax-candle. In 1845, when recalling his reporting days, he informed Forster that he " had to charge for all sorts of breakages fifty times in a journey without question," as the ordinary results of the pace he was compelled to travel. He had charged his employers for everything but a broken head, " which," he naïvely added, " is the only thing they would have grumbled to pay for." One of the foremost of these expeditions took place in 1835, when he and a colleague, Thomas Beard, journeyed by express coach to Bristol to report, for the *Morning Chronicle*, the political speeches in connection with Lord John

Russell's Devon contest. He lodged at the Bush Inn, where that "ill-starred gentleman," Mr. Winkle, took up his quarters when fleeing from the wrath of the infuriated Dowler, as set forth in the thirty-eighth chapter of "Pickwick." We are told that Mr. Winkle found Bristol "a shade more dirty than any place he had ever seen"; that, at the time referred to (nearly eighty years ago), the pavements of that city were "not the widest or cleanest upon earth," its streets were "not altogether the straightest or least intricate," and their "manifold windings and twistings" greatly puzzled Mr. Winkle, who, when exploring them, lost his way, with the result that he unexpectedly came upon his old acquaintances, Bob Sawyer and Ben Allen, the former occupying a newly-painted tenement (not identified), which had been recently converted into "something between a shop and a private house," with the word "Surgery" inscribed above the window of what had been the front parlour. At the Bush tavern the fugitive was discovered by Sam Weller, who had received peremptory orders from "the governor" to follow and keep him in sight until Mr. Pickwick arrived on the scene. The Bush no longer exists; it stood in Corn Street, near the Guildhall, and was taken down in 1864, the present Wiltshire Bank marking the site. It will be remembered that it was to Clifton, on the outskirts of Bristol, where Arabella Allen was sent by her brother (who regarded himself as "her natural protector and guardian") to spend a few months at an old aunt's, "in a nice dull place," in order to break her to his will that she should marry Bob Sawyer ("late Nockemorf"). Hither Sam Weller went in quest of her, walking (as we are told) "up one street and down another—we were going to say, up one hill and down another, only it's all uphill at Clifton"—and, after struggling across the Downs, "against a good high wind," eventually arrived at "several little villas of quiet and secluded appearance," at one of which he, too, met a familiar acquaintance in "the pretty housemaid from Mrs. Nupkins's," who proved a valuable guide to the whereabouts of Miss Allen. In 1866 and 1869 Dickens gave public readings at Clifton, staying on the former occasion at the Down Hotel. The suspension bridge across the Avon is the old Hungerford Bridge, removed in 1863, and the sight of it at the time of his later visits to Clifton must have recalled to Dickens the troubled period of his boyhood at the blacking factory.

The occasion of the Bristol reporting expedition in 1835 is also memorable for the fact that it marks the date of Dickens's first visit to the contiguous city of Bath, which plays a still more important part in the Transactions of the Pickwick Club. At Bath he had to prepare a report of a political dinner given there by Lord John Russell, and to despatch it " by Cooper Company's Coach, leaving the Bush (Bristol) at half-past six next morning." It was sharp work, as Russell's speech at the banquet had to be transcribed by Dickens for the printers while travelling by the mail-coach viâ Marlborough for London ; this necessitated for himself and Thomas Beard the relinquishment of sleep and rest during two consecutive days and nights. It is fair to suppose that on one of his early reporting expeditions to the West of England Dickens put up for a night at the quaint little roadside inn near Marlborough Downs, which he so carefully describes in the Bagman's Story in " Pickwick."

" It was a strange old place, built of a kind of shingle, inlaid, as it were, with cross-beams, with gable-topped windows projecting over the pathway, and a low door with a dark porch, and a couple of steep steps leading down into the house, instead of the modern fashion of half a dozen shallow ones leading up to it." Like Tom Smart, the hero of the story, he doubtless slept in the selfsame apartment, with its " big closets, and a bed which might have served for a whole boarding-school, to say nothing of a couple of oaken presses that would have held the baggage of a small army." Nay, he may even have experienced Tom Smart's strange hallucination in regard to the ancient armchair, apparently assuming in the uncertain light of the chamber fire the outlines of a strangely-formed specimen of humanity, although probably he did not go so far as to enter into con-versation with this remarkable bedroom companion, as did the Bagman, whose vivid imagination, aided by the narcotic effects of his noggins of whisky, enabled him to impart a spiciness to his narrative. From the detailed manner in which Dickens portrays this old-fashioned alehouse, we are justified in con-jecturing that such a place really existed during the thirties, and attempts have been made to identify it, for we need not take for granted the statement in " Pickwick" that the place had been pulled down. From inquiries which I instituted on the subject, a local correspondent informs me that the Marquis of Ailesbury's Arms at Clatford somewhat answered to the description prior to extensive structural altera-tions effected about twenty years ago.

Another investigator considers that the inn at Beckhampton, the Catherine Wheel, fulfils most of the requirements. With this conclusion, however, the Rev. W. H. Davies, of Avebury, is not disposed to agree, and the late Rev. A. C. Smith, in his "British and Roman Antiquities," tells us that the inn which formerly existed at Shepherd's Shord (or Shore) was the one referred to by Dickens, and that at the time of the publication of "Pickwick" everybody in Wiltshire so identified it. Another suggestion is that the original of Tom Smart's house of call was the Kennett Inn at Beckhampton, which, according to a drawing of the place, answers the descriptions even better than those already mentioned, although it stood upon the wrong side of the road. We ought, I think, to accept the local opinion of Pickwickian days, and fix the scene of the Bagman's adventure at Shepherd's Shore.*

Remembering what little leisure he must have had in the midst of political turmoil and journalistic responsibilities while at Bath, it is indeed surprising to find how truthful a presentment of that delightful city is achieved in "Pickwick." On the occasion in question he put up at a small hotel, the Saracen's Head, a quaint-looking, unpretentious building still existing in Broad Street, its two red-tiled gables and stuccoed front facing that thoroughfare. The landlady relates that Dickens, owing to the fact that all the bedrooms of the house were occupied on his arrival at a late hour, had to be accommodated with a room over some stables or outbuildings at the farther end of the inn yard, overlooking Walcot

* These interesting conjectures are culled from the *Wiltshire Advertiser*, February 4, 1904.

Street.* Visitors are shown a curious two-handled mug which the novelist is believed to have used, and the bedroom once occupied by him, and containing the old four-post bedstead upon which he slept ; while in another room, low and raftered, is to be seen the stiff wooden armchair in which he sat !— relics that are deservedly cherished and handed down as heirlooms.

Bath is frequently referred to in the novelist's writings, and, judging by a particular allusion to the historic town, it seems not to have left a very favourable impression on his mind, for he there mentions it as "that grass-grown city of the ancients."† At a subsequent date he remarked : "Landor's ghost goes along the silent streets here before me. . . . The place looks to me like a cemetery which the dead have succeeded in rising and taking. Having built streets of their old gravestones, they wander about scantly trying to ' look alive.' A dead failure."‡ He had a pleasant remembrance of Walter Savage Landor at No. 35, St. James's Square, upon which a tablet was fixed in 1903 recording the fact of a visit paid to him by the novelist on the latter's birthday, February 7, 1840, on which occasion he was accompanied by Mrs. Dickens, Maclise, and Forster, the party remaining there until the end of the month. We are assured by his biographer that it was during this visit to Bath "that the fancy which was shortly to take the form of Little Nell first occurred to its author." The girl-heroine of " The Old Curiosity Shop " was an immense favourite with Landor, who

* " The Real Dickens Land," by H. Snowden Ward, 1903.
† " Bleak House," chap. lvi.
‡ Letter to Forster, January 27, 1869.

MILE END COTTAGE, ALPHINGTON. (*Page* 94.)

Taken by Dickens in 1839 or his parents' use. "The house is on the high road to Plymouth, and the situation is
charming" (letter to Mr. Thomas Mitton).

in after-years emphatically declared that the one mistake of his life was that he had not purchased the house in which the conception of her dawned upon Dickens, and then and there burned it to the ground, so that no meaner associations should desecrate it.

Brief as his stay in Bath undoubtedly was in the capacity of reporter for the *Morning Chronicle* in 1835, he, nevertheless, made excellent use of his abnormal powers of observation in spite of professional activities, his retentive memory enabling him to reproduce in "The Pickwick Papers" a few months afterwards those typical scenes in the social life of Bath of that period, which has since undergone many changes, Mr. Pickwick being almost the last to witness the peculiarities of Bath society as described by the novel-writers of a century or so ago. Dickens noticed, among other topographical features, the steepness of Park Street, which (he said) " was very much like the perpendicular streets a man sees in a dream, which he cannot get up for the life of him." He remembered, too, that the White Hart Hotel (the proprietor of which establishment was the Moses Pickwick who owned the very coach on which Sam Weller saw inscribed " the magic name of Pickwick ") stood " opposite the great Pump Room, where the waiters, from their costume, might be mistaken for Westminster boys, only they destroy the illusion by behaving themselves so much better."* The White Hart flourished in Stall Street, and until 1864 (when the house was given up) the waiters wore knee-breeches and silk stockings, and the women servants donned neat muslin caps. The old coach-

* " The Pickwick Papers," chap. xxxiv.

ing inn, alas! no longer exists, and its site is indicated by the Grand Pump Room Hotel, the original carved sign of a white hart being preserved and still used over the door of an inn of the same name in Widcombe, a suburb of Bath.

The pen-pictures of scenes at the Assembly Rooms and Pump Rooms are admirably rendered in the pages of " Pickwick," and we feel convinced that the author must have witnessed them.

" Bath being full, the company and the sixpences for tea poured in in shoals. In the ball-room, the long card-room, the octagonal card-room, the staircases, and the passages, the hum of many voices and the sound of many feet were perfectly bewildering. Dresses rustled, feathers waved, lights shone, and jewels sparkled. There was the music— not of the quadrille band, for it had not yet commenced, but the music of soft, tiny footsteps, with now and then a clear, merry laugh, low and gentle, but very pleasant to hear in a female voice, whether in Bath or elsewhere. Brilliant eyes, lighted up with pleasurable expectations, gleamed from every side ; and look where you would, some exquisite form glided gracefully through the throng, and was no sooner lost than it was replaced by another as dainty and bewitching.

" In the tea-room, and hovering round the card-tables, were a vast number of queer old ladies and decrepit old gentlemen, discussing all the small-talk and scandal of the day, with a relish and gusto which sufficiently bespoke the intensity of the pleasure they derived from the occupation. Mingled with these groups were three or four matchmaking mammas, appearing to be wholly absorbed by the conversation in which they were taking part, but failing not from time to time to cast an anxious sidelong glance upon their daughters, who, remembering the maternal injunction to make the best of their youth, had already commenced incipient flirtations in the mislaying of scarves, putting on gloves, setting down cups, and so forth—slight matters apparently, but which may be turned to surprisingly good account by expert practitioners.

"Lounging near the doors, and in remote corners, were various knots of silly young men, displaying various varieties of puppyism and stupidity, amusing all sensible people near them with their folly and conceit, and happily thinking themselves the objects of general admiration—a wise and merciful dispensation which no good man will quarrel with.

"And, lastly, seated on some of the back benches, where they had already taken up their positions for the evening, were divers unmarried ladies past their grand climacteric, who, not dancing because there were no partners for them, and not playing cards lest they should be set down as irretrievably single, were in the favourable situation of being able to abuse everybody without reflecting on themselves. In short, they could abuse everybody, because everybody was there. It was a scene of gaiety, glitter, and show, of richly-dressed people, handsome mirrors, chalked floors, girandoles, and wax-candles ; and in all parts of the scene, gliding from spot to spot in silent softness, bowing obsequiously to this party, nodding familiarly to that, and smiling complacently on all, was the sprucely-attired person of Angelo Cyrus Bantam, Esquire, Master of the Ceremonies" (chap. xxxv.).

" The great pump-room is a spacious saloon, ornamented with Corinthian pillars, and a music gallery, and a Tompion clock, and a statue of Nash, and a golden inscription, to which all the water-drinkers should attend, for it appeals to them in the cause of a deserving charity. There is a large bar with a marble vase, out of which the pumper gets the water; and there are a number of yellow-looking tumblers, out of which the company gets it; and it is a most edifying and satisfactory sight to behold the perseverance and gravity with which they swallow it. There are baths near at hand, in which a part of the company wash themselves; and a band plays afterwards to congratulate the remainder on their having done so. There is another pump-room, into which infirm ladies and gentlemen are wheeled, in such an astonishing variety of chairs and chaises that any adventurous individual who goes in with the regular number of toes is in imminent danger of coming out without them; and there is a third, into which the quiet people go, for it is less noisy than either. There is an immensity of promenading, on crutches and off, with sticks and without, and a great deal of conversation, and liveliness, and pleasantry. . . . At the afternoon's promenade . . . all the great people, and all the morning water-drinkers, meet in grand assemblage. After this, they walked out or drove out, or were pushed out in bath-chairs, and met one another again. After this, the gentlemen went to the reading-rooms and met divisions of the mass. After this, they went home. If it were theatre night, perhaps they met at the theatre; if it were assembly night, they met at the rooms; and if it were neither, they met the next day. A very pleasant routine, with perhaps a slight tinge of sameness" (chap. xxxvi.).

The citizens of Bath are naturally proud of its Pickwickian associations; Mr. Pickwick's lodging in the Royal Crescent is pointed out, as well as the actual spot in the Assembly Rooms where he played whist, while the veritable rout seats of that time are preserved and cherished. The Royal Hotel, whence Mr. Winkle hurriedly departed by coach for Bristol, has shared the fate of the White Hart; indeed, Mr. Snowden Ward avers that there was no Royal Hotel in Bath in Dickens's time, and that he probably refers to the York House Hotel, frequently patronized by royalty, and once at least by the novelist himself. We may still look, however, upon the "small greengrocer's shop" where Bath footmen used to hold their social evenings, and memorable as the scene of the "leg-o'-mutton swarry." It is now the Beaufort Arms, in a narrow street out of Queen's Square, Bath, and within a short distance of No. 12 in the Square, the residence of Angelo Cyrus Bantam, Esq., Master of the Ceremonies, who welcomed Mr. Pickwick to Ba-ath.

In the course of an interesting speech delivered in 1865 at the second annual dinner of the Newspaper Press Fund, Dickens made an interesting allusion to the Devonshire political contest of thirty years previously, and to the part he took in it as a *Chronicle* reporter. "The very last time I was at Exeter," he said, "I strolled into the Castle yard, there to identify, for the amusement of a friend, the spot on which I once 'took,' as we used to call it, an election speech of Lord John Russell . . . in the midst of a lively fight maintained by all the vagabonds in that division of the county, and under such a pelting rain that I remember two good-natured colleagues, who chanced to be at leisure, held a pocket-handkerchief over my note-book, after the manner of a state canopy in an ecclesiastical procession." In 1839 a mission of a very different character caused him to journey to " the capital of the West " (as that city has been denominated), his object being to arrange a new home for his parents in that locality. Making his headquarters at the New London Inn (where he had Charles Kean's sitting-room), he soon discovered a suitable residence about a mile south from the city boundary on the highroad to Plymouth, Mile End Cottage, which is really divided into two portions, one-half being then occupied by the landlady, and the other being available for the new tenants. Dickens, when writing to Forster, described the place as " two white cottages," and respecting the accommodation here provided for his parents, he said : " I almost forget the number of rooms, but there is an excellent parlour, which I am furnishing as a drawing-room, and there is a splendid garden." In a letter to his friend Thomas Mitton he dilates more fully upon the attractions of the cottage and its environment. " I do assure you," he observed, " that I am charmed with the place and the beauty of the country round about, though I have not seen it under very favourable circumstances. . . . It is really delightful, and when the house is to rights and the furniture all in, I shall be quite sorry to leave it. . . . The situation is charming ; meadows in front, an orchard running parallel to the garden hedge, richly-wooded hills closing in the prospect behind, and, away to the left, before a splendid view of the hill on which Exeter is situated, the cathedral towers rising up into the sky in the most picturesque manner possible. I don't think I ever saw so cheerful and pleasant a spot. . . ."* It will be remembered that " Nicholas Nickleby " opens with a reference to " a sequestered part of the county of Devonshire " (sic), where lived one Mr. Godfrey Nickleby, the grandfather of the hero of the story ; and there is no doubt that the home of Mrs. Nickleby's friends, the Dibabses, as pictured by that lady in the fifty-fifth chapter, was identical with the tenement in which Mr. and Mrs. John Dickens found a temporary lodgment—" the beautiful little thatched white house one story high, covered all over with ivy and creeping plants, with an exquisite little porch with twining honeysuckle, and all sorts of things."

Charles Dickens's return to England at the end of his triumphant progress through the United States in 1842 was the occasion for a special celebration, which assumed the form of a holiday trip in Cornwall with his cherished friends Stanfield, Maclise, and Forster. They chose Cornwall for the excursion because it transpired that this " desolate region," as Dickens termed it, was unfamiliar to them, and would there-fore enhance their enjoyment. The decision to make Cornwall their destination suggested to Dickens the idea of opening his new book, " Martin Chuzzlewit," on that rugged coast, "in some terrible dreary, iron-bound spot," and to select the lantern of a lighthouse (probably the Longship's, off Land's End) as the opening scene ; but he changed his mind. This expedition in the late summer lasted nearly three weeks, it proving a source of such unexpected

* " The Letters of Charles Dickens."

and unabated attraction that the merry party felt loath to return to town. Railways were not of much use to them, as they did not penetrate to the remote districts which the travellers desired to visit. Post-horses were therefore requisitioned, and when the roads proved inaccessible to these, pedestrianism was perforce resorted to. They visited Tintagel, and explored every part of mountain and sea " consecrated by the legends of Arthur." They ascended to the cradle of the highest pinnacle of Mount St. Michael,* and descended in several mines ; but above all the marvels of land and sea, that which yielded the most lasting impression was a sunset at Land's End, concerning which Forster says : " There was something in the sinking of the sun behind the Atlantic that autumn afternoon, as we viewed it together from the top of the rock projecting farthest into the sea, which each in his turn declared to have no parallel in memory." The famous Logan Stone, too, was not forgotten. Writing subsequently to Forster, the novelist said : " Don't I still see the Logan Stone, and you perched on the giddy top, while we, rocking it on its pivot, shrank from all that lay concealed below !" For Forster possessed the necessary courage and agility (lacking in the rest) to mount the huge swaying stone, the feat being immortalized by Stanfield in a sketch bequeathed to the Victoria and Albert Museum.† Lastly, the waterfall at St.

* ". . . A strong place perched upon the top of a high rock, around which, when the tide is in, the sea flows, leaving no road to the mainland."—"A Child's History of England," chap. ix.

In the early part of the last century the Logan, or Rocking, Stone could be easily swayed to and fro, its poise being so accurate that a hand-push would set it in motion and cause it to rock. In April, 1824, this huge rock was overthrown by a

THE GEORGE INN, AMESBURY. (*Page* 100.)

" The Blue Dragon" of " Martin Chuzzlewit."

Wighton was visited, memorable for the fact that a painting of it (from a sketch made on this occasion) appears as the background to Maclise's picture of " A Girl at a Waterfall," the figure being depicted from a sister-in-law of Dickens. The novelist, while the glow of enjoyment was yet upon him, could not resist dilating upon the exhilarating effect induced by this glorious holiday in the midst of natural scenery, then witnessed by the joyous quartette for the first time ; and the following letter, addressed to his American friend, Professor Felton, fittingly concludes these references to the event which he ever recalled with delight : " Blessed star of the morning, such a trip as we had into Cornwall, just after Longfellow went away ! . . . We went down into Devonshire by the railroad, and there we hired an open carriage from an innkeeper, patriotic in all Pickwick matters, and went on with post-horses. Sometimes we travelled all night, sometimes all day, sometimes both. I kept the joint-stock purse, ordered all the dinners, paid all the turn-pikes, conducted facetious conversations with the post-boys, and regulated the pace at which we travelled. Stanfield (an old sailor) consulted an enormous map on all disputed points of wayfaring, and referred, moreover, to a pocket-compass and other scientific instruments. The luggage was in Forster's depart-ment, and Maclise, having nothing particular to do,

---

party of sailors, and, filled with remorse for this foolish act, the leader of the party (Lieutenant Goldsmith, nephew of the poet) determined to replace it at his own expense, the stone being swung back with pulleys to its original resting-place in November of the same year, amid great local rejoicing. But its rocking propensities were sadly diminished, and at the present time have ceased altogether.

sang songs. Heavens! if you could have seen the
necks of bottles — distracting in their immense
varieties of shape—peering out of the carriage
pockets! If you could have witnessed the deep
devotion of the post-boys, the wild attachment of the
hostlers, the maniac glee of the waiters! If you
could have followed us into the earthy old churches
we visited, and into the strange caverns on the
gloomy seashore, and down into the depths of
mines, and up to the tops of giddy heights, where
the unspeakably green water was roaring I don't
know how many hundred feet below! If you could
have seen but one gleam of the bright fires by which
we sat in the big rooms of ancient inns at night until
long after the small hours had come and gone, or
smelt but one steam of the hot punch, . . . which
came in every evening in a huge, broad, china bowl!
I never laughed in my life as I did on this journey.
It would have done you good to hear me. I was
choking and gasping and bursting the buckle off the
back of my stock all the way, and Stanfield . . . got
into such apoplectic entanglements that we were often
obliged to beat him on the back with portmanteaus
before we could recover him. Seriously, I do believe
that there never was such a trip. And they made
such sketches, those two men, in the most romantic
of our halting-places, that you could have sworn we
had the Spirit of Beauty with us, as well as the Spirit
of Fun. . . ."*

Dickens, as already intimated, originally conceived
the idea of opening the tale of "Martin Chuzzlewit"
on the coast of Cornwall. Instead of this, however,
we find, in the initial chapter of that story, that the

* "The Letters of Charles Dickens."

scene is laid in a village near Salisbury. That he
had previously made himself acquainted with Wiltshire is indicated in his correspondence with Forster
in 1842, where he declared (for instance) that in
beholding an American prairie for the first time he
felt no such emotions as he experienced when crossing
Salisbury Plain. "I would say to every man who
can't see a prairie," he remarked, "go to Salisbury
Plain, Marlborough Downs, or any of the broad,
high, open lands near the sea. Many of them are
fully as impressive, and Salisbury Plain is *decidedly*
more so."

Six years later he and Forster, with John Leech
and Mark Lemon, procured horses at Salisbury, and
"passed the whole of a March day in riding over
every part of the plain, visiting Stonehenge, and
exploring Hazlitt's hut at Winterslow, the birthplace
of some of his finest essays." *

There are persons still living in the neighbourhood of Salisbury who remember Dickens's quest for
local colour with which to give a semblance of reality
to his topographical descriptions in "Chuzzlewit."
"The fair old town of Salisbury" figures prominently in that story, and we must believe that his
allusion (in the fifth chapter) to the grand cathedral
derived inspiration from personal observation: "The
yellow light that streamed in through the ancient
windows in the choir was mingled with a murky
red. As the grand tones (of the organ) resounded
through the church, they seemed to Tom to find
an echo in the depth of every ancient tomb, no less
than in the deep mystery of his own heart." He
makes a curious mistake in the twelfth chapter when

* Forster's "Life of Dickens."

speaking of the "towers" of the old cathedral ; but, of course, he knew perfectly well that the venerable fane is surmounted by a beautifully tapering spire, immortalized in one of Constable's most remarkable pictures.   The scene in Salisbury Market, so vividly portrayed in chapter v., could not have been penned except by an acute observer like Dickens ; nothing escaped him, and he noted all the details of that busy scene, and stored them in his retentive memory in readiness for the pen-picture which he afterwards delineated so faithfully and so picturesquely.

The "little Wiltshire village," described as being within an easy journey of Salisbury, has not been absolutely identified.   Certain commentators opine that Amesbury is intended, while others consider it more probable that the novelist had in his mind the village of Alderbury, and that its principal inn, the Green Dragon, was the original of Mrs. Lupin's establishment, concerning which that unprincipled adventurer, Montague Tigg, spoke with undisguised disparagement and contempt.

CHAPTER V.

IN SOUTHERN ENGLAND.

PORTSMOUTH is justly proud of the fact that it is the native place of certain distinguished men—to wit, Charles Dickens, Sir Walter Besant, and Brunel the great engineer.

In 1838, when engaged upon "Nicholas Nickleby," Dickens renewed acquaintance with the town, of which it is fair to suppose he could remember but little, seeing that he was only about two years of age when his father was recalled to London, taking with him wife and family. He, however, astonished Forster (who accompanied him thither) by readily recalling memories of his childhood there, and distinctly remembering such details as the exact shape of the military parade.

Dickens's particular object in then journeying to Portsmouth (not on foot, as did Nicholas and Smike) was doubtless for the express purpose of obtaining local colour for "Nickleby," as presented in chapters xxiii. and xxiv. He succeeded in finding suitable lodging for Vincent Crummles at Bulph the pilot's in St. Thomas's Street (conjectured to be No. 78), for Miss Snevellicci at a tailor's in Lombard Street, while Nickleby and his companion were quartered at a tobacconist's on the Common Hard, which he describes as "a dirty street leading down to the dockyard." The old Portsmouth Theatre, the scene of Nicholas's early triumphs on the stage, plays a prominent part in the tale. This primitive building, which stood in the High Street, was destroyed many years ago ; it occupied the site of the Cambridge Barracks ; the present house is styled "The New Theatre Royal." The story is current in Portsmouth that Dickens, on the occasion just referred to, called upon the manager at the old theatre and actually asked for a small part. Whether this tradition be true or false, we are justified in assuming that he and Forster went behind the scenes and chatted with the players, the result being the portrayal of those inimitable descriptions which treat of the company of Mr. Vincent Crummles, and of the " great bespeak " for Miss Snevellicci. Apropos of the theatre itself, as it appeared to the hero of the story, we read : " It was not very light, but Nicholas found himself close to the first entrance on the prompter's side, among bare walls, dusty scenes, mildewed clouds, heavily daubed draperies, and dirty floors. He looked about him ; ceiling, pit, boxes, gallery, orchestra, fittings, and decorations of every kind—all looked coarse, cold, gloomy, and wretched. ' Is this a theatre?' whispered Smike in amazement. ' I thought it was a blaze of light and finery.' ' Why, so it is,' replied Nicholas, hardly less surprised ; ' but not by day, Smike—not by day!'" Matters theatrical have improved vastly since then, and provincial theatres now vie with those in the Metropolis in regard to the comfort and magnificence of their appointments.

Plymouth, in a much less degree, is also associated
with Dickens. There are slight references to the town
in "David Copperfield" and "Bleak House." He
visited Plymouth in 1858 and in 1861, staying at
the West Hoe Hotel on the first occasion, when he
gave public readings in a handsome room at Stone-
house, "on the top of a windy and muddy hill,
leading (literally) to nowhere ; and it looks (except
that it is new and *mortary*) as if the subsidence of the
waters after the Deluge might have left it where it
is."* In 1861 we find Plymouth again included in
the itinerary of an Autumn Reading tour. Dickens's
connection with Brighton was of a more intimate
character, his acquaintance with "the Queen of
watering-places" beginning as early as 1837, when
he resumed the writing of "Oliver Twist." "We
have a beautiful bay-windowed sitting-room here,
fronting the sea," he informed Forster ; "but I have
seen nothing of B.'s brother who was to have shown
me the lions, and my notions of the place are consequently somewhat confined, being limited to the
pavilion, the chain pier, and the sea. The last is
quite enough for me. . . ." During his stay he
attended a performance at the theatre of a comedy
entitled "No Thoroughfare," this being, curiously
enough, the exact title of the only story he ever
took part himself in dramatizing three years before
his death. In 1841 he again journeyed by coach,
the Brighton Era, to Brighton, and busied himself
there with "Barnaby Rudge," making his temporary
home at the Old Ship Hotel at No. 38, King's
Road—not the more modern establishment of that

* "The Letters of Charles Dickens."

name in Ship Street.*   In May, 1847, Dickens
lodged for some weeks at No. 148, King's Road,
for the recovery of his wife's health after the birth
of a son, christened Sydney Smith Haldemand.   He
went there first with Mrs. Dickens and her sister
and the eldest boy (the latter just recovered from an
attack of scarlet fever), and was joined at the latter
part of the time by his two little daughters.   In the
spring of 1850 he was again at the King's Road
lodgings, his thoughts being then concentrated upon
the new weekly journal, *Household Words*, the first
number of which appeared in March of that year.

In March, 1848, Dickens and his wife, accompanied by Mrs. Macready, spent three weeks in
Brighton at Junction House, where they were " very
comfortably (not to say gorgeously) accommodated";
and for a short time during the spring of 1853,
when engaged upon " Bleak House," he rented
rooms at No. 1, Junction Parade.   Of all his
Brighton residences, however, that which justly
claims priority is the celebrated Bedford Hotel,
whence (in November, 1848) we find letters addressed
to his friends Frank Stone, A.R.A. (who was then
designing illustrations for " The Haunted Man ")
and Mark Lemon.   To the artist he said : " The
Duke of Cambridge is staying at this house, and
they are driving me mad by having Life Guards
bands under our windows playing *our* overtures (*i.e.*,
the overtures in connection with the amateur performances by Dickens and his friends) ! . . . I
don't in the abstract approve of Brighton.   I couldn't

* Thackeray wrote some of the early numbers of "Vanity Fair"
at the Old Ship Inn, and caused George Osborne and his bride
to spend the first few days of their married life there.

AMESBURY CHURCH. (*Page* 100.)

Where Tom Pinch played the organ for nothing, and Mr. Pecksniff heard himself
denounced.

pass an autumn here, but it is a gay place for a week or so; and when one laughs or cries, and suffers the agitation that some men experience over their books, it's a bright change to look out of window, and see the gilt little toys on horseback going up and down before the mighty sea, and thinking nothing of it."* In February, 1849, Dickens spent another holiday at Brighton, accompanied by his wife and sister-in-law and two daughters, and they were joined by the genial artist John Leech and his wife. They had not been in their lodgings a week when both his landlord and his landlord's daughter went raving mad, this untoward circumstance compelling the lodgers to seek quarters elsewhere—at the Bedford Hotel. "If," wrote Dickens, when relating the adventure to Forster, "you could have heard the cursing and crying of the two; could have seen the physician and nurse quoited out into the passage by the madman at the hazard of their lives; could have seen Leech and me flying to the doctor's rescue; could have seen our wives pulling us back; could have seen the M.D. faint with fear; could have seen three other M.D.'s come to his aid; with an atmosphere of Mrs. Gamps, strait-waist-coats, struggling friends and servants, surrounding the whole, you would have said it was quite worthy of me, and quite in keeping with my usual proceedings." The Reading tour in 1861 again took him to Brighton and the Bedford, and one of his

* "The Letters of Charles Dickens." This passage reminds us of the following contemporary reference in "Vanity Fair," chap. xxii.: "But have we any leisure for a description of Brighton?—for Brighton, a clean Naples, with genteel lazzaroni; for Brighton, that always looks brisk, gay, and gaudy, like a harlequin's jacket. . . ."

audiences included the Duchess of Cambridge and a Princess. " I think they were pleased with me, and I am sure I was with them."

Apart from these personal associations, Brighton derives particular interest from the fact that it figures largely in " Dombey and Son." It was at the Bedford where Mr. Dombey stayed during his week-end visits to Brighton for the purpose of seeing his children, and where Major Bagstock enjoyed the privilege of dining with that purse-proud City merchant. It was to Brighton that Little Paul was sent to school, first as a pupil of the austere and vinegary Mrs. Pipchin. " The castle of this ogress and child-queller was in a steep by-street at Brighton, where the soil was more than usually chalky, flinty, and sterile, and the houses were more than usually brittle and thin ; where the small front-gardens had an unaccountable property of producing nothing but marigolds, whatever was sown in them ; and where snails were constantly discovered holding on to the street doors, and other public places they were not expected to ornament, with the tenacity of cupping-glasses." Here also was the superior and " very expensive " establishment of Dr. Blimber —" a great hot-house, in which there was a forcing apparatus incessantly at work," where, we are told, " mental green peas were produced at Christmas, and intellectual asparagus all the year round. Mathematical gooseberries (very sour ones, too) were common at untimely seasons, and from mere sprouts of bushes, under Dr. Blimber's cultivation. Every description of Greek and Latin vegetable was got off the driest twigs of boys under the frostiest circumstances." We learn on excellent authority that Dr. Blimber and his school really existed at Brighton, the prototype of the worthy pedagogue being Dr. Everard, whose celebrated seminary was familiarly called the "Young House of Lords," from the aristocracy of the pupils. It seems that during the Christmas holidays it became customary with Dr. Everard to organize dances for the boys (such as that so delightfully described in the fourteenth chapter of "Dombey and Son"). In those days, curly locks were considered an indispensable accessory to full dress, and the whole of the afternoon preceding the ball Dr. Everard's house was pervaded by a strong smell of singed hair and curling-tongs.* "There was such . . . a smell of singed hair that Dr. Blimber sent up the footman with his compliments, and wished to know if the house was on fire."

In the summer and autumn of 1849 Dickens went with his family, for the first time, to Bonchurch, Isle of Wight, where he hired for six months the attractive villa, Winterbourne, belonging to the Rev. James White (an author of some repute and a keen lover of books), with whom his intimacy, already begun, now ripened into a lifelong friendship. The novelist had in June of that year passed a brief period at Shanklin, whence he wrote to his wife : "I have taken a most delightful and beautiful house, belonging to White, at Bonchurch—cool,

* *Vide* "Mary Boyle—Her Book," 1901. Miss Boyle, an intimate friend of Dickens, pleasingly records her recollections of Dr. Everard's school, where, as a girl, she was very popular among his pupils, and much in request at the dances. Her partners included the late and the present Lords Northampton, Mr. Frederick Leveson-Gower, and her cousins, the sons of Sir Augustus Clifford.

airy, private bathing ; everything delicious.   I think
it is the prettiest place I ever saw in my life at home
or abroad. . . .   A waterfall in the grounds, which
I have arranged with a carpenter to convert into a
perpetual shower-bath."*

He liked the place exceedingly at first, and considered that the views from the summit of the
highest downs " are only to be equalled on the
Genoese shore of the Mediterranean."   The variety
of walks in the neighbourhood struck him as extraordinary ; the people were civil, and everything was
cheap, while he fully appreciated the fact that the
place was certainly cold rather than hot in the summer-
time, and the sea-bathing proved " delicious."   Here
at Bonchurch he was joined by John Leech, and
soon settled down to work, being then engaged upon
the early portion of " David Copperfield," varying
his literary occupations by taking part, with his
customary zest, in dinners at Blackgang and picnics
of " tremendous success " on Shanklin Down.   One
of these festivities he particularly remembered, when
he expressly stipulated that the party should be provided with materials for a fire and a great iron pot
to boil potatoes in, these, with the comestibles, being
conveyed to the ground in a cart.   Doubtless this
was the veritable function described by the late
Mrs. Phœbe Lankester ("Penelope").   Her husband,
Dr. Lankester (to whom Dickens referred as " a
very good, merry fellow "), and other distinguished
men of science then staying at Sandown, belonged to
a select and notable club founded originally by the
younger members of the British Association, and

* " The Letters of Charles Dickens."

called the "Red Lions." The Bonchurch party, headed by Dickens, constituted themselves into a temporary rival club, called the "Sea Serpents," and picnics were arranged between the two factions, the meetings usually taking place at Cook's Castle. "Well do I recollect," observes Mrs. Lankester, "the jolly procession from Sandown as it moved across the Downs, young and old carrying aloft a banner bearing the device of a noble red lion painted in vermilion on a white ground. Wending up the hill from the Bonchurch side might be seen the 'Sea Serpents,' with their ensign floating in the wind—a waving, curling serpent, cut out of yards and yards of calico, and painted of a bronzy-green colour with fiery red eyes, its tail being supported at the end by a second banner-holder. Carts brought up the provisions on either side, and at the top the factions met to prepare and consume the banquet on the short, sweet grass under shadow of a rock or a tree. Charles Dickens delighted in the fun. He usually boiled the potatoes when the fire had been lighted by the youngsters, and handed them round in a saucepan, and John Leech used to make sketches of us, one of which is still to be seen in the collection from *Punch*, and is called 'Awful Appearance of a "Wopps" at a Picnic.'* I was very young then, and did not fully realize what it was to eat potatoes boiled by Charles Dickens, or to make a figure in a sketch by Leech." On one of these jovial occasions a race was run, after the repast, between Mark Lemon and Dr. Lankester, both competitors of abnormal stoutness, Macready officiating as judge,

* See *Punch*, August 25, 1849. In the background of the drawing are represented the ruins of Cook's Castle.

after which the merry party adjourned to Dickens's villa for tea and music.

His stay at Bonchurch was enlivened, too, by visits from such cherished friends as Justice Talfourd, Frank Stone, and Augustus Egg, social intercourse with whom formed agreeable interludes between severe spells of literary work. Unhappily, the enervating effect of the climate presently began to prostrate him, and after a few weeks' residence he complained of insomnia, extreme mental depression, and a "dull, stupid languor." Commenting upon his physical condition, he remarked: "It's a mortal mistake—that's the plain fact. Of all the places I ever have been in, I have never been in one so difficult to exist in pleasantly. Naples is hot and dirty, New York feverish, Washington bilious, Genoa exciting, Paris rainy ; but Bonchurch—smashing. I am quite convinced that I should die here in a year." His wife, sister-in-law, and the Leeches were also affected, but not to the same extent, and, finding it impossible to endure much longer the distressing symptoms, he determined to leave Bonchurch at the end of September and "go down to some cold place," such as Ramsgate, for a week or two, hoping thus to shake off the effects. In the interval he completed the fifth number of "Copperfield," after which, during the remainder of the holiday, he and his party (by way of relaxation) indulged in such amusements as "great games of rounders every afternoon, with all Bonchurch looking on." These revels were disagreeably interrupted by a serious accident to John Leech, who, while bathing in a rough sea, was knocked over by an immense wave, which resulted in congestion of

the brain, and necessitated, first, the placing of
"twenty of his namesakes on his temple," and then,
as the illness developed, the continuous application
of ice to the head, with blood-letting from the arm.
The unfortunate artist becoming gradually worse,
Dickens essayed the effect of mesmerism, in the
virtue of which he apparently had faith, and succeeded
in obtaining a period of much-needed sleep for the
relief of the invalid, whose condition thenceforth
improved until complete restoration of his customary
health became assured, enabling him for many subsequent years to delight the world with his inimitable
pencil.   As already intimated, Dickens remained in
the Island until the expiration of the time originally
planned for this seaside holiday; but although he
brought away many happy associations, he never
renewed acquaintance with Bonchurch.

CHAPTER VI.

IN EAST ANGLIA.

DICKENS must have become first acquainted with Eastern England during his reporting days, as many of the scenes in "Pickwick" are laid in the chief town of Suffolk. The merging, in 1899, of the *Suffolk Chronicle* into the *Suffolk Times and Mercury* revived an incident in Dickens's career as a reporter, in stating that it was the *Suffolk Chronicle* which, in 1835, brought him down to Ipswich for the purpose of assisting in reporting the speeches in connection with the Parliamentary election at that time being contested in the county. We are further assured by the same authority that "Boz" (then actually engaged upon the opening chapters of "Pickwick") stayed at the Great White Horse in Tavern Street for two or three weeks, and it has been reasonably surmised that the night adventure with "the middle-aged lady in the yellow curl-papers," ascribed to Mr. Pickwick, was a veritable experience of the young author himself. It is said that, in consequence of this embarrassing mischance, Dickens entertained a feeling of prejudice against the house, and never liked the place afterwards. If this be correct, it accounts for the somewhat disparaging remarks in "Pickwick" concerning the hotel: "Never were

THE COMMON HARD, PORTSMOUTH. (*Page* 102.)

Nickleby and Smike lodged "at a tobacconist's shop on the Common Hard," now known as "The Old Curiosity Shop."

such labyrinths of uncarpeted passages, such clusters of mouldy, badly-lighted rooms, such huge numbers of small dens for eating or sleeping in, beneath any one roof, as are collected together between the four walls of the Great White Horse at Ipswich." Nevertheless, the famous hostelry still flourishes, and makes the most of its Pickwickian associations, even to the extent of revealing to visitors the identical bedroom (No. 16), where the adventure occurred. Over the principal hotel entrance we may yet see the stone presentment of a "rampacious" white horse, "distantly resembling an insane cart-horse"; but the building generally has since been altered in the direction of certain improvements necessitated by the requirements of present-day travellers.*

We can readily conceive that the description of the coach journey to Ipswich, starting from the Bull Inn, Whitechapel, and rattling along the Whitechapel and Mile End Roads, "to the admiration of the whole population of that pretty densely-populated quarter," and so to Suffolk's county town (as duly set forth in the twenty-second chapter of "Pickwick"), is a personal reminiscence of Dickens himself when fulfilling his engagement with the *Suffolk Chronicle*.

While busy with newspaper responsibilities, to which he had pledged himself, he evidently made the best use of the opportunities thus afforded of noting certain topographical details of the town, finding "in a kind of courtyard of venerable appearance," near St. Clement's Church, a suitable locale for the incident of the unexpected meeting of Sam

* In March, 1902, the Great White Horse was sold by public auction, and purchased by the lessee for £14,500.

Weller and Job Trotter ; the " green gate," which
Job was seen to open and close after him, is locally
believed to be one that adjoins the churchyard a few
yards from Church Street, the inhabitants taking
great pride in pointing it out as the precise spot
where Alfred Jingle's body-servant embraced Sam
"in an ecstasy of joy."   In regard to these scenes
Ipswich is mentioned by name, but it has been conjectured that the town also figures in " Pickwick "
under the successful disguise of "Eatanswill," although
Norwich has been mentioned in this connection.
Certainly the weight of such evidence as that prof-
fered by the *Suffolk Times and Mercury* favours the
belief that Ipswich stood for the unflattering portrait,
and, but for the facts as averred by that journal, we
should possibly never have had Mr. Pickwick's
nocturnal misadventure, nor heard of the rival editors
of the *Eatanswill Gazette* and the *Eatanswill Inde-
pendent*.

Dickens's reporting expedition in Suffolk during
the electoral campaign of 1835 doubtless compelled
him to include in his itinerary several of the leading
towns in the county, where political meetings would
naturally be held, and among them Bury St. Edmunds, where, according to tradition, he put up at
the Angel Inn, his room being No. 11. In describing
this hostelry, Mr. Percy Fitzgerald says that it is "a
solemn, rather imposing, and stately building, of a
gloomy slate colour, and of the nature of a family
hotel. . . . It has yards and stabling behind it,
which must have flourished in the old posting times."
Standing in Market Square, it continues to this day
to be the principal hotel in the place, and remains in
much the same condition as when the novelist knew

it about seventy years ago. Bury St. Edmunds, like Ipswich, has won immortality in the pages of " Pickwick," where it is referred to as " a handsome little town of thriving and cleanly appearance," its well-paved streets being specially commended. In one of " The Uncommercial Traveller " papers he calls it " a bright little town."

We are told that the coach, with Mr. Pickwick among the passengers newly arrived from Eatanswill, pulled up at the " large inn, situated in a wide, open street, nearly facing the old abbey." " And this," said Mr. Pickwick, " is the Angel. We alight here, Sam . . . ;" whereupon a private room was ordered, and then dinner, everything being arranged with caution, for it will be remembered that Mr. Pickwick and his faithful attendant were in quest of that thorough-paced adventurer Alfred Jingle, Esq., " of No Hall, Nowhere," intent upon frustrating probable intentions on his part of practising further deceptions. Here, at Bury, the " Mulberry man " (otherwise Job Trotter) was found by Sam in the pious act of reading a hymn-book, a discovery which proved to be the initial stage of Mr. Pickwick's adventure at the boarding-school for young ladies— Westgate House—which, we are told, is a well-known residence called Southgate House, although there are other antique-looking schools for girls on the Westgate side of the town that seem more or less to answer the description.

More than two decades later—*i.e.*, in 1861— Dickens again visited both Ipswich and Bury St. Edmunds, when he gave readings from his works, beginning the series at Norwich, where, writing from the recently-demolished Royal Hotel in the Market

Place, he spoke of his audience in that city as " a very lumpish audience indeed . . . an intent and staring audience. They laughed, though, very well, and the storm made them shake themselves again. But they were not magnetic, and the great big place (St. Andrew's Hall) was out of sorts somehow."*

On the last day of the year 1848, Dickens contemplated an excursion with Leech, Lemon, and Forster to some old cathedral city then unfamiliar to him, believing the sight of " pastures new " would afford him the necessary mental refreshment. "What do you say to Norwich and Stanfield Hall ?" he queried of Forster, and it was decided forthwith that the three friends should depart thence. Stanfield Hall had just gained unenviable notoriety as the scene of a dreadful tragedy—the murder of Jeremy, the Recorder of Norwich, by Rush, afterwards executed at Norwich Castle. They arrived between the Hall and Potass Farm as the search was going on for the pistol, and the novelist was fain to confess that the place had nothing attractive about it, unless such a definition might be applied to a " murderous look that seemed to invite such a crime."

Quaint old Norwich, as it has been justly termed (although its quaintness and picturesqueness have suffered woefully in recent years through commercial innovations), did not appeal to Dickens, who declared it to be " a disappointment "—everything there save the ancient castle, "which we found fit for a gigantic scoundrel's exit," alluding, of course, to Rush. The castle no longer serves as the county prison, and its gruesome associations are practically obliterated by the wholesome use to which the

* " The Letters of Charles Dickens."

massive Norman structure is devoted, that of museum and art gallery under civic control.

Without doubt Dickens's principal motive in journeying to Norfolk and Suffolk in 1848 was to obtain " local colour " for " David Copperfield," the writing of which he was then meditating. He stayed for a time at Somerleyton Hall, near Lowestoft, as the guest of Sir Morton Peto, the well-known civil engineer and railway contractor, under whose guidance he first made acquaintance with that portion of Suffolk, studying it carefully, and afterwards portraying it in the story with characteristic exactitude. Two miles from Somerleyton Hall (now the residence of Sir Saville Crossley, M.P.) is Blundeston, a typical English village, which, thinly disguised as Blunderstone, appears in the book as the birthplace of David. The novelist afterwards confessed that he noticed the name on a direction-post between Lowestoft and Yarmouth, and at once adapted it because he liked the sound of the word ; the actual direction-post still standing as he saw it.

There is a little uncertainty respecting the identity of the " Rookery " where David first saw the light, the Rectory being regarded by some careful students of the topography of " Copperfield " as the possible original, whence can be obtained a fairly distinct view of the church porch and the gravestones in the churchyard. Local tradition, however, favours Blundeston Hall, the present tenant-owner of which (Mr. T. Hardwich Woods) remembers that when very young he was taken by the old housekeeper down the "long passage . . . leading from Peggotty's kitchen to the front entrance," and shown the "dark storeroom" opening out of it. While staying in the neighbourhood Dickens visited Blundeston Hall, which presented a weird and gloomy appearance before its recent restoration, and the fact is recalled that for a brief space he contemplated the prospect from one of the side windows facing the church, then plainly visible from this point, but the view is now obstucted by trees.

" In no other residence hereabouts," observes Mr. Woods, " do rooms and passages coincide so exactly with the descriptions given in the novel." In the garden we may still behold the " tall old elm-trees " in which there were formerly some rooks' nests, but no rooks. ("David Copperfield all over !" cried Miss Betsey. " David Copperfield from head to foot ! Calls a house a rookery when there's not a rook near it, and takes the birds on trust because he sees the nests !")

The roadside tavern referred to in the fourth chapter as " our little village alehouse " may be recognised in the Plough at Blundeston, to the recently-stuccoed front of which are affixed the initials " R. E. B." and the date " 1701 " in wrought-iron.

Blundeston Church, like many others in East Anglia, has a round tower (probably Norman), but no spire, as mentioned in the story; the high-backed pews and quaint pulpit have since been replaced by others of modern workmanship, but happily the ancient rood-screen with its painted panels has survived such sacrilegious treatment. The porch, with a sun-dial above the entrance, is still intact. "There is nothing," says little David, " half so green that I know anywhere as the grass of that churchyard ; nothing half so shady as its trees ;

nothing half so quiet as its tombstones. The sheep are feeding there when I kneel up, early in the morning, in my little bed in a closet within my mother's room to look out at it; and I see the red light shining on the sun-dial, and I think within myself, 'Is the sun-dial glad, I wonder, that it can tell the time again?'" It is interesting to know that it was at Blundeston House (now called The Lodge) where the poet Gray stayed with his friend the Rev. Norton Nicholls (rector of the adjoining parishes of Lound and Bradwell), and here he found that sublime quietude which his soul loved.

That popular seaside resort, Great Yarmouth, was first seen by Dickens at the close of 1848, and he thought it "the strangest place in the wide world, one hundred and forty-six miles of hill-less marsh between it and London"; substituting the word "country" for "marsh," the statement would be practically correct. Strongly impressed by the exceptional and Dutch-like features of this flat expanse, on the eastern margin of which stands the celebrated seaport, he forthwith decided to "try his hand" at it, with the result (as everyone knows) that he placed there, on the open Denes, the home of Little Em'ly and the Peggottys. In all probability the idea of causing them to live in a discarded boat arose from his having seen a humble abode of this character when perambulating the outskirts of Yarmouth, for such domiciles were not uncommon in those days, and might be met with both in Yarmouth and Lowestoft; indeed, we are told that even now the little village of Carracross, on the west coast of Ireland, consists of seventeen superannuated fishing-boats, one of which dates from about 1740. Apropos

of Peggotty's boat, it may be remarked that the old
inverted boat, bricked up and roofed in, which revealed itself in 1879 during the process of demolition,
has hitherto been considered as the veritable domicile
immortalized in "Copperfield"; but the cherished
belief is not worthy of credence, being unsupported
by trustworthy evidence, an important point antago-
nistic to that conjecture being the fact that Peggotty's
boat stood on the open Denes upon its keel ("Phiz"
notwithstanding), whereas that discovered in Tower
Road was put keel uppermost, by a shrimper, on
garden ground in the midst of a noisome locality
called by the inappropriate name "Angel's Piece,"
with no "sandy waste" surrounding it.*

At Yarmouth Dickens made his headquarters at
the Royal Hotel, on the sea-front, having John
Leech and Mark Lemon as congenial companions,
for illness prevented Forster from remaining with
them. The old town, and the flat, sandy expanse of
uncultivated land between river and sea, already
alluded to as the Denes, deeply imprinted itself upon
Dickens's mental retina, and he conveys his impressions thereof through the medium of his boy-hero :

"It looked rather spongy and sloppy, I thought,
as I carried my eye over the great dull waste that
lay across the river; and I could not help wondering,
if the world were really as round as my geography
book said, how any part of it came to be so flat.

* For this information I am indebted to Dr. John Bately, of
Gorleston, who has made a careful study of the subject, and to
whom I am similarly obliged for useful suggestions respecting
"Blunderstone Rookery," the original of which (he is convinced) is the Rectory, not the Hall. Is it not probable that
Dickens combined the features of both places, and so produced
a composite portrait ?

THE GEORGE, GRETA BRIDGE. (*Page* 123.)

Dickens visited this inn when collecting material for " Nicholas Nickleby," and here Mr. Squeers alighted from the coach on his return from London with the new boys.

But I reflected that Yarmouth might be situated at one of the poles, which would account for it.

"As we drew a little nearer, and saw the whole adjacent prospect lying a straight low line under the sky, I hinted to Peggotty that a mound or so might improve it, and also that if the land had been a little more separated from the sea, and the town and the tide had not been quite so much mixed up, like toast-and-water, it would have been nicer. . . .

"When we got into the street (which was strange enough to me), and smelt the fish, and pitch, and oakum, and tar, and saw the sailors walking about, and the carts jingling up and down over the stones, I felt that I had done so busy a place an injustice, and said as much to Peggotty, who . . . told me it was well known . . . that Yarmouth was, upon the whole, the finest place in the universe."

David, as Ham carried him on his broad back from the carrier's cart to the boathouse, gazed upon the dreary amplitude of the Denes in anxious expectation of catching a glimpse of the romantic abode for which they were destined. "We turned down lanes," he says, "bestrewn with bits of chips and little hillocks of sand, and went past gasworks, rope-walks, boat-builders' yards, shipwrights' yards, ship-breakers' yards, caulkers' yards, riggers' lofts, smiths' forges, and a great litter of such places, until we came out upon the dull waste I had already seen at a distance. . . . I looked in all directions, as far as I could stare over the wilderness, and away at the sea, and away at the river, but no house could I make out "—nothing except a "ship-looking thing," which presently resolved itself into the identical house for which they were bound, and proved to be—in the boy's estimation, at least—as charming and delightful as Aladdin's palace, " roc's egg and all." It is pointed out by Dr. Bately that the description given by Dickens (as above quoted) of the various objects seen on the way from Yarmouth to the South Denes really reverses their order, just as he noted them when walking in the contrary direction. There are not many boat-builders' yards now remaining hereabouts.

CHAPTER VII.

IN THE NORTH.

IN 1837 Dickens's thoughts were concentrated upon a new serial story, " Nicholas Nickleby," in which he determined to expose the shortcomings of cheap boarding-schools then flourishing in Northern England, his first impressions of which were picked up when, as a child, he sat " in by-places, near Rochester Castle, with a head full of Partridge, Strap, Tom Pipes, and Sancho Panza." The time had arrived (he thought) when, by means of his writings, he could secure a large audience, to whom he might effectively present the actual facts concerning the alleged cruelties customarily practised at those seminaries of which he had heard so much. Having thus resolved to punish the culprits by means of his powerful pen, and, if possible, to suppress the evils of the system they favoured, the novelist and his illustrator, " Phiz," departed from London by coach on a cold winter's day in January, 1838, for Greta Bridge, in the North Riding, with the express intention of obtaining authoritative information regarding the subject of the schools, for in that locality were situated some of the most culpable of those institutions. Greta Bridge takes its name from a lofty bridge of one arch, erected on the line of Watling

Street, upon the site of a more ancient structure, over the river Greta, a little above its junction with the Tees.

The parish of Rokeby, in the petty sessional division of Greta Bridge, is celebrated as the scene of Sir Walter Scott's poem, " Rokeby," which was written on the spot, and does no more than justice to the beautiful scenery of the neighbourhood.

Dickens and " Phiz " broke their journey at Grantham, at which town they arrived late on the night of January 30, and put up at the George— " the very best inn I have ever put up at." Early the next morning they continued their journey by the Glasgow mail, " which charged us the remarkably low sum of £6 fare for two places inside." Snow began to fall, and the drifts grew deeper, until there was " no vestige of a track " over the wild heaths as the coach approached the destination of the two fellow-travellers, who were half frozen on their arrival at Greta Bridge. In the story the author gives the name of the hostelry where Squeers and his party alighted from the coach as the George and New Inn ; but, in so doing, he indulges in an artistic license, for he thus bestows upon one house the respective signs of two distinct inns at Greta Bridge, situated about half a mile from each other. The George stands near the bridge already referred to, the public portion of the premises having since been converted into a private residence. The New Inn has also been changed, and is now a farmhouse called Thorpe Grange ; built before the railway era for Mr. Morrit, the landlord of the George, it not only rivalled the older establishment, but absorbed its custom, the owner claiming it as the veritable inn of Dickens's story.* It seems very probable that the novelist himself put up at the New Inn during his brief tour of investigation in 1838 ; writing thence to his wife at this date, he said that at 11 p.m. the mail reached " a bare place with a house standing alone in the midst of a dreary moor, which the guard informed us was Greta Bridge. I was in a perfect agony of apprehension, for it was fearfully cold, and there were no outward signs of anybody being up in the house. But to our great joy we discovered a comfortable room, with drawn curtains and a most blazing fire. In half an hour they gave us a smoking supper and a bottle of mulled port (in which we drank your health), and then we retired to a couple of capital bedrooms, in each of which there was a rousing fire halfway up the chimney. We have had for breakfast toast, cakes, a Yorkshire pie, a piece of beef about the size and much the shape of my portmanteau, tea, coffee, ham and eggs, and are now going to look about us. . . ."† After exploring the immediate neighbourhood, Dickens, accompanied by " Phiz," went by post-chaise to Barnard Castle, four miles from Greta Bridge, and just over the Yorkshire border, there to deliver a letter given to him by Mr. Smithson (a London solicitor, who had a York-shire connection), and to visit the numerous schools thereabouts. This letter of introduction bore refer-ence (as the author explains in his preface to " Nicholas Nickleby ") to a supposititious little boy who had been left with a widowed mother who didn't know what to do with him ; the poor lady had

* The Morrit Arms is now the only establishment of the kind in Greta Bridge.

† " Letters of Charles Dickens."

thought, as a means of thawing the tardy compassion of her relations on his behalf, of sending him to a Yorkshire school. " I was the poor lady's friend, travelling that way ; and if the recipient of the letter could inform me of a school in his neighbourhood, the writer would be very much obliged." The result of this " pious fraud " (as Dickens himself termed it) has become a matter of history. The person to whom the missive was addressed was a farmer (since identified as John S——, of Broadiswood), who appears in the story as honest John Browdie. Not being at home when the novelist called upon him, he journeyed through the snow to the inn where Dickens was staying, and entreated him to advise the widow to refrain from sending her boy to any of those wretched schools " while there's a harse to hoold in a' Lunnun, or a goother to lie asleep in !" The old coaching-house where this memorable interview is believed to have taken place was the still existing Unicorn at Bowes. Another inn associated with this tour of inspection is the King's Head, Barnard Castle,* where Dickens made a brief stay, and where he observed, across the way, the name of " Humphreys, clockmaker," over a shop door, this suggesting the title of his next work, " Master Humphrey's Clock."

It was at Bowes where he obtained material which served him for depicting the " internal economy " of Dotheboys Hall, in the school presided over by William Shaw, who, it has since transpired, was by no means the worst of his tribe. As a matter of fact, he won respect from his neighbours, and is remem-

* The King's Head, in the Market Place, Barnard Castle, has been enlarged since 1838, but the older portion remains much as it was then.

bered by many of his pupils (some of whom attained high positions in various professions) as a worthy and much injured man. In "Nicholas Nickleby," however, he became a scapegoat for others who thoroughly deserved the punishment inflicted upon Shaw. Even to-day many of the people at Bowes regard Dickens's attack as unjust so far as that particular schoolmaster is concerned, and visitors to the place are advised to refrain from alluding to Dotheboys Hall.

There is no lack of evidence to prove the general accuracy of the novelist's description, and to him we owe a deep debt of gratitude for so successful an attempt to annihilate those terrible " Caves of Despair." Bowes is situated high up on the moorland, and may now be reached by railway from Barnard Castle. The village consists principally of one street nearly three-quarters of a mile in length, running east to west, and is lighted with oil lamps, under a village lighting committee. Shaw's house (known generally as Dotheboys Hall until recent times) stands at the western extremity of Bowes. The present tenants have altered somewhat the original appearance of the house by attempting to convert it into a kind of suburban villa—in fact, it is now called "The Villa." Prior to these structural changes it was a long, low building of two storeys. The classroom and dormitories were demolished a few years ago, but the original pump, at which Shaw's pupils used to wash, is still in the yard at the back of the house, and an object of great interest to tourists.

Nearly all provincial towns in England were visited by Dickens during his acting and reading tours, and many can boast of more intimate relations with the novelist. It was from Liverpool, on January 4, 1842, that he embarked on board the *Britannia* for the United States—his first memorable visit to Transatlantic shores—and in 1844 he presided at a great public meeting held in the Mechanics' Institution, then sadly in need of funds, on which occasion he delivered a powerful speech in support of the objects of that foundation. Referring to the building, he said : " It is an enormous place. The lecture-room . . . will accommodate over thirteen hundred people. . . . I should think it an easy place to speak in, being a semicircle with seats rising one above another to the ceiling."

Respecting this function, we learn from a contemporary report that long before the hour appointed for the opening of the doors the street was crowded with persons anxious to obtain admission, so anxious were they to see and hear the young man (then only in his thirty-third year) who had given them " Pickwick," " Oliver Twist," and " Nicholas Nickleby." At the termination of his speech a vote of thanks was accorded to the novelist, who, in replying thereto, concluded his acknowledgments by quoting the words of Tiny Tim, " God bless us every one." An interesting incident lay in the fact that the young lady who presided at the pianoforte was Miss Christina Weller, who, with her father, was introduced to the author of " Pickwick," thus causing considerable merriment.

In 1847 Dickens and his distinguished company of amateur actors gave a representation in Liverpool of Ben Jonson's comedy, " Every Man in His Humour," for the benefit of Leigh Hunt. The

DOTHEBOYS HALL, BOWES. (*Page* 126.)

Visited by Dickens when writing "Nicholas Nickleby."

Reading tours in the fifties and sixties again called him to that busy mercantile centre, one of the readings taking place in St. George's Hall—" the beautiful St. George's Hall," as he described it : " brilliant to see when lighted up, and for a reading simply perfect." One of the closing incidents of his life was the great Liverpool banquet, which took place on April 10, 1869, in St. George's Hall, after his country Readings, the late Marquis of Dufferin presiding, the function being made memorable by an eloquent speech by the novelist, replying to a remonstrance from Lord Houghton against his (Dickens's) objection to entering public life.* While sojourning at Liverpool he usually stayed at the Adelphi Hotel. In 1844 he made Radley's Hotel his headquarters.

It is quite in accordance with our expectations to find frequent mention of Liverpool throughout Dickens's works. For descriptive passages we must turn to the pages of " Martin Chuzzlewit " and certain of his minor writings, where we discover interesting and important references " to that rich and beautiful port," as he calls it in one instance. Apropos of the return to England of Martin Chuzzlewit the younger and his faithful companion Mark Tapley after their trying experiences in the New Country, the novelist, in thus depicting Liverpool and the Mersey, doubtless records his own impressions of some two years previous on his arrival there at the termination, in 1842, of his American tour :

" It was mid-day and high-water in the English port for which the *Screw* was bound, when, borne in gallantly upon the fulness of the tide, she let go her anchor in the river.

* See " The Speeches of Charles Dickens."

" Bright as the scene was—fresh, and full of motion ; airy, free, and sparkling—it was nothing to the life and exaltation in the hearts of the two travellers at sight of the old churches, roofs, and darkened chimney-stacks of home. The distant roar that swelled up hoarsely from the busy streets was music in their ears ; the lines of people gazing from the wharves were friends held dear ; the canopy of smoke that overhung the town was brighter and more beautiful to them than if the richest silks of Persia had been waving in the air. And though the water, going on its glistening track, turned ever and again aside to dance and sparkle round great ships, and heave them up, and leaped from off the blades of oars, a shower of diving diamonds, and wantoned with the idle boats, and swiftly passed, in many a sporting chase, through obdurate old iron rings, set deep into the stonework of the quays, not even it was half so buoyant and so restless as their fluttering hearts, when yearning to set foot once more on native ground."

In one of " The Uncommercial Traveller " papers (1860) will be found this vivid pen-picture of the slums of Liverpool, favoured by seafaring men of the lower class, a district probably little altered since those lines were penned :

" A labyrinth of dismal courts and blind alleys, called ' entries,' kept in wonderful order by the police, and in much better order than by the Corporation, the want of gaslight in the most dangerous and infamous of these places being quite unworthy of so spirited a town. . . . Many of these sailors' resorts we attained by noisome passages so profoundly dark that we felt our way with our hands. Not one of the whole number we visited was without its show of prints and ornamental crockery, the quantity of the latter, set forth on little shelves and in little cases in otherwise wretched rooms, indicating that Mercantile Jack must have an extraordinary fondness for crockery to necessitate so much of that bait in his traps . . . etc."*

With the characteristics of that other great Lancashire town, Manchester, the novelist became, perhaps, even more intimate. "Manchester is (*for* Manchester) bright and fresh," he wrote to Miss Hogarth from the Queen's Hotel in 1869, where he stayed on the occasion of his Farewell Readings in the provinces, and where the chimney of his sitting-room caught fire and compelled him to "turn out elsewhere to breakfast." Long before this date—that is, in 1843 —the people of Manchester were first privileged to meet him on the occasion of a bazaar in the Free Trade Hall in aid of the fund for improving the financial condition of the Athenæum, then sadly in debt. The bazaar was followed by a soirée, held in the same building, under the presidency of Dickens, who then delivered a speech which has been described as "a masterpiece of graceful eloquence." The subject thereof forcibly appealed to him—viz., the education of the very poor, for he did not believe in the old adage that averred a little learning to be a "dangerous thing," but rather that the most minute particle of knowledge is preferable to complete and consummate ignorance. This memorable function is noteworthy also by reason of the fact that among the speakers who addressed the vast

* "Poor Mercantile Jack," in *All the Year Round*, March 10, 1860.

audience were Disraeli and Cobden. Dickens expressed a wish to become a member of the Athenæum, but left Manchester without going through the necessary formalities—an oversight soon rectified, however.

In 1852, on the occasion of the inauguration of the Manchester Public Free Libraries, the novelist accepted an invitation to be present at an important meeting held at Campfield, the "first home" of these free libraries (formerly known as "The Hall of Science"); the meeting was attended by a number of distinguished men, including Bulwer Lytton, Thackeray, John Bright, Peter Cunningham, etc., and it naturally fell to Dickens to make a speech, having the use of literature as its theme. Thackeray, by the way, had prepared a careful oration, but, after delivering half a sentence, ignominiously sat down! Public oratory was not his forte. In 1858 Dickens presided at the annual meeting of the Institutional Association of Lancashire and Cheshire, held in the Manchester Athenæum and the Free Trade Hall, and handed prizes to candidates from more than a hundred local mechanics' institutes affiliated to the association. "Knowledge has a very limited power indeed," he observed, in the speech delivered on behalf of the Manchester Mechanics' Institute in Cooper Street, "when it informs the head alone; but when it informs the head and heart too, it has power over life and death, the body and the soul, and dominates the universe." We are reminded that this peroration is an echo of words in "Hard Times" (written four years previously), and that his exhortation to the Manchester audience practically reproduced the leading thought in that powerful novel—

a story which impelled the admiration of Ruskin, who, commenting upon it, said that the book "should be studied with close and earnest care by persons interested in social questions." In " Hard Times " Manchester is disguised as matter-of-fact Coketown, and the presentment is easily recognisable :

" It was a town of red brick, or of brick that would have been red if the smoke and ashes had allowed it ; but, as matters stood, it was a town of unnatural red and black, like the painted face of a savage. It was a town of machinery and tall chimneys, out of which interminable serpents of smoke trailed themselves for ever and ever, and never got uncoiled. It had a black canal in it, and a river that ran purple with evil-smelling dye, and vast piles of building full of windows, where there was a rattling and a trembling all day long, and where the piston of the steam-engine worked monotonously up and down, like the head of an elephant in a state of melancholy madness. It contained several large streets, all very like one another, and many small streets, still more like one another, inhabited by people equally like one another, who all went in and out at the same hours, with the same sound upon the same pavements, to do the same work, and to whom every day was the same as yesterday and to-morrow, and every year the counterpart of the last and the next. These attributes of Coketown were in the main inseparable from the work by which it was sustained ; against them were to be set off comforts of life which found their way all over the world, and elegancies of life which made we will not ask how much of the fine lady, who could scarcely bear to hear the place mentioned. You saw nothing in Coketown but what was severely workful. . . .

"In the hardest working part of Coketown; in the innermost fortifications of that ugly citadel, where Nature was as strongly bricked out as killing airs and gasses were bricked in; at the heart of the labyrinth of narrow courts upon courts, and close streets upon streets, which had come into existence piecemeal, every piece in a violent hurry for some one man's purpose, and the whole one unnatural family, shouldering, and trampling, and pressing one another to death; in the last close nook of the great exhausted receiver, where the chimneys, for want or air to make a draught, were built in an immense variety of stunted and crooked shapes, as though every house put out a sign of the kind of people who might be expected to be born in it."

Of Coketown on a sunny midsummer day (for "there was such a thing sometimes, even in Coketown") the author exhibits a realistic picture. "Seen from a distance in such weather, Coketown lay shrouded in a haze of its own, which appeared impervious to the sun's rays. You only knew the town was there because you knew there could have been no such sulky blotch upon the prospect without a town. A blur of soot and smoke, now confusedly bending this way, now that way, now aspiring to the vault of heaven, now murkily creeping along the earth as the wind rose and fell or changed its quarter—a dense, formless jumble, with sheets of cross-light in it, that showed nothing but masses of darkness. Coketown in the distance was suggestive of itself, though not a brick of it could be seen . . .

the streets were hot and dusty on the summer day, and the sun was so bright that it even shone through the heavy vapour drooping over Coketown, and could not be looked at steadily. Stokers emerged from low underground doorways and factory yards, and sat on steps, and posts, and palings, wiping their swarthy visages, and contemplating coals. The whole town seemed to be frying in oil. There was a stifling smell of hot oil everywhere. The steam-engines shone with it ; the dresses of the Hands were soiled with it ; the mills throughout their many stories oozed and trickled it. The atmosphere of those Fairy palaces* was like the breath of the simoon, and their inhabitants, wasting with heat, toiled languidly in the desert. But no temperature made the melancholy-mad elephants more mad or more sane. Their wearisome heads went up and down at the same rate, in hot weather and cold, wet weather and dry, fair weather and foul. The measured motion of their shadows on the walls was the substitute Coketown had to show for the shadows of rustling woods ; while for the summer hum of insects it could offer, all the year round, from the dawn of Monday to the night of Saturday, the whir of shafts and wheels.

"Drowsily they whirred all through this sunny day, making the passenger more sleepy and more hot as he passed the humming walls of the mills. Sun-blinds and sprinklings of water a little cooled the main streets and shops, but the mills and the courts and the alleys baked at a fierce heat. Down upon the river, that was black and thick with dye,

* Elsewhere in the book the author tells us that the great factories looked like Fairy palaces when illumined at night.

some Coketown boys, who were at large—a rare sight there—rowed a crazy boat, which made a spurious track upon the water as it jogged along, while every dip of an oar stirred up vile smells."*

Apropos of "Hard Times," it may be mentioned that in 1854 Dickens stayed at the Bull Hotel in Preston, when he visited that town expressly for the purpose of witnessing the effects of a strike in a manufacturing town. He failed, however, to secure much material here for the story, for he wrote: "Except the crowds at the street-corners reading the placards *pro* and *con*, and the cold absence of smoke from the mill-chimneys, there is very little in the streets to make the town remarkable." He expected to find in Preston a model town, instead of which it proved to be, in his estimation, a "nasty place," while to the Bull he referred in disrespectful terms as an "old, grubby, smoky, mean, intensely formal red-brick house, with a narrow gateway and a dingy yard." Preston figures in the early chapters of "George Silverman's Explanation," a cellar in that town being the birthplace of the principal character, the Rev. George Silverman.

Reverting to Manchester, it must not be forgotten

* The late Mr. Robert Langton, author of "The Childhood and Youth of Charles Dickens," states that Dickens, in "Hard Times," is unsuccessful in his attempt to render the Lancashire dialect—that the utterances put into the mouths of Stephen Blackpool and others in the book "are very far from being correct," a matter upon which, from his long residence in Manchester, that critic is qualified to speak. Mr. Langton points out that the inscription on the sign of the Pegasus' Arms, at which inn Sleary's circus company put up, "Good malt makes good beer," etc., was taken from an old sign, the Malt Shovel, existing until 1882 at the foot of Cheetham Hill.

THE RED LION, BARNET. (*Page* 173.)

Dickens and Forster dined here in March, 1838, to celebrate the birth of Miss Mary (Mamie) Dickens.

that Dickens, in the capacity of an actor, journeyed thither four times, appearing with his amateur company first at the Theatre Royal in 1847 for the benefit of Leigh Hunt, twice in 1852 at the Old Free Trade Hall, and again in that building in 1857. Needless to say, the performances attracted vast and enthusiastic audiences, and were eminently successful both artistically and financially.

The Free Trade Hall, too, was the scene of his public Readings in Manchester, and it is recorded that he was accustomed to stay at Old Trafford as the guest of Mr. John Knowles, of the Theatre Royal. This large house was then surrounded by an extensive wood, and considered to be a lonely and remote place, but is now near a network of railways, and the reverse of rural.*

About the year 1841 Charles Dickens's elder sister Fanny (nearly two years his senior) married Henry Burnett, an accomplished operatic singer, who had retired from performing on the stage, and taken up his abode in Manchester as an instructor in music, Mrs. Burnett, herself a musician of considerable acquirements, assisting her husband in conducting the choir of Rusholme Road Congregational Chapel, where they worshipped, and the pastor of which was the Rev. James Griffin, who has recorded in print his recollections of the Burnetts. There is, consequently, a link of a distinctly personal kind connecting Dickens with Manchester, which is made additionally interesting by the fact that the little

* See the *Manchester Evening Chronicle*, January 7, 1904. In this paper were published during 1903-1904 a series of interesting articles on "Dickens and Manchester," whence some of these details are culled.

crippled son of the Burnetts (who lived in Upper Brook Street) was the prototype of Paul Dombey. It may be added that Mr. Burnett unconsciously posed for some of the characteristics of Nicholas Nickleby, while in Fanny Dorrit there are certain indications suggesting that her portrait was inspired by the novelist's sister.

In a literary sense, Manchester can boast of other Dickensian associations, for here resided the originals of the delightful Cheeryble Brothers, who (the author assures us in his preface to "Nicholas Nickleby") were "very slightly and imperfectly sketched" from life. "Those who take an interest in this tale," he adds, "will be glad to learn that the Brothers Cheeryble live; that their liberal charity, their singleness of heart, their noble nature, and their unbounded benevolence, are no creation of the author's brain, but are prompting every day (and oftenest by stealth) some munificent deed in that town of which they are the pride and honour." The actual models whence he portrayed the Cheerybles with approximate accuracy were the brothers Grant, William and Daniel, merchants, of Ramsbottom and Manchester, with whom the novelist declared he "never interchanged any communication in his life." From evidence recently forthcoming, however, we learn that in 1838 (the year prior to the publication of "Nickleby") he and Forster were the guests of Mr. Gilbert Winter, of Stocks House, Cheetham Hill Road, Manchester, to whom they went with a letter of introduction from Harrison Ainsworth. Stocks House (demolished in 1884) was formerly surrounded by a moat, a portion of which was filled up at the time of the construction of the old road to

Bury, the fine old mansion probably representing the manor-house of Cheetham Manor, given as a reward to the Earls of Derby after the Battle of Bosworth Field. It was at Stocks House that Dickens became acquainted with the Grants; indeed, Forster practically admits this when he says: " A friend now especially welcome was the novelist Mr. Ainsworth, with whom we visited, during two of those years (1838 and 1839), friends of art and letters in his native Manchester, from among whom Dickens brought away the Brothers Cheeryble. . . ." The Rev. Hume Elliot informs us that although William and Daniel Grant had residences in Manchester, they preferred to live together at Springside, Ramsbottom, " which they made a veritable home of hospitality and good works,"* and it is fair to assume that Dickens must have seen at their home the original of David, " the apoplectic butler," or ascertained from an authentic source the peculiarities of Alfred, who served the Grants in a like capacity and possessed similar idiosyncrasies.

There are two houses in Manchester associated with the Grants. One of these, now a parcel-receiving office of the London and North-Western Railway Company, is in Mosley Street, and the other (a more important place) stands at the lower end of Cannon Street (No. 15), a large, roomy warehouse, occupied by a paper dealer, who caused the name " Cheeryble House " to be placed on the front of the building.†

* " The County of the Cheerybles," by the Rev. Hume Elliot.

† Many of these details are quoted from the *Manchester Evening News*, October 27, 1903.

The rare combination of the qualities of charity and humanity with sound business instincts, such as are ascribed to the Cheeryble Brothers, was exactly true of the Grants. On the death of William Grant (the elder brother) in 1842, the novelist (writing from Niagara Falls to his American friend, Professor Felton), said : " One of the noble hearts who sat for the Cheeryble Brothers is dead. If I had been in England I would certainly have gone into mourning for the loss of such a glorious life. His brother is not expected to survive him. [He died in 1855, at the age of seventy-five.] I am told that it appears from a memorandum found among the papers of the deceased that in his lifetime he gave away £600,000, or three million dollars." There is a marble tablet to the memory of William Grant in St. Andrew's Presbyterian Church, Ramsbottom, recording his " vigour of understanding, his spotless integrity of character, and his true benevolence of heart. . . . If you are in poverty," the inscription continues, " grieve for the loss of so good a friend ; if born to wealth and influence, think of the importance of such a trust, and earn in like manner by a life of charitable exertion the respect and love of all who knew you, and the prayers and blessings of the poor." Honoured descendants of the two philanthropists are still surviving in the city which cherishes their memory.

In 1847 the novelist presided at a meeting of the Mechanics' Institute in Leeds, thus proving his practical interest in the welfare of working men—an interest again testified in 1855, when he visited Sheffield for the purpose of reading the " Christmas Carol " in the Mechanics' Hall on behalf of the funds of the Institute in that busy town. After the reading, the Mayor begged his acceptance of a handsome service of table cutlery and other useful articles of local manufacture, the gift of a few gentlemen in Sheffield, as a substantial manifestation of their gratitude to him.

In a letter to Wilkie Collins, dated August 29, 1857, Dickens said : " I want to cast about whether you and I can go anywhere—take any tour—see anything — whereon we could write something together. Have you any idea tending to any place in the world ? Will you rattle your head and see if there is any pebble in it which we could wander away and play at marbles with?" This was written just after the conclusion of the readings and theatrical performances in aid of the Douglas Jerrold fund, Dickens experiencing a sense of restlessness when the excitement attending them had subsided, and seeming anxious "to escape from himself" by means of a pilgrimage with a congenial companion, and such as might provide material for a series of papers in *Household Words*. Arrangements were speedily made with this object, and the two friends started forthwith "on a ten or twelve days' expedition to out-of-the-way places, to do (in inns and coast corners) a little tour in search of an article and in avoidance of railroads." They decided for a foray upon the fells of Cumberland, Dickens having discovered (in " The Beauties of England and Wales " and other topographical works) descriptions of "some promising moors and bleak places thereabout." To the Lake district they accordingly departed in September, and their adventures are related in " The Lazy Tour of Two Idle Apprentices" (published in *Household Words* during the latter part of the same year), the authors skilfully collaborating in the preparation of the record, nearly all the descriptive passages emanating from the pen of Dickens. Almost the first thing attempted by the travellers was the climbing of Carrock Fell, "a gloomy old mountain 1,500 feet high." "Nobody goes up," said Dickens to Forster; "guides have forgotten it." The proprietor of a little inn, however, volunteered his services as guide, and the party of enthusiasts ascended in a downpour of rain. The Two Idle Apprentices (who bear the respective names Francis Goodchild and Thomas Idle, the former being the pseudonym favoured by Dickens) concluded that to perform the feat "would be the culminating triumph of Idleness." "Up hill and down hill, and twisting to the left, and with old Skiddaw (who has vaunted himself a great deal more than his merits deserve, but that is rather the way of the Lake country) dodging the apprentices in a picturesque and pleasant manner. Good, weatherproof, warm, pleasant houses, well white-limed, scantily dotting the road. . . . Well-cultivated gardens attached to the cottages. . . . Lonely nooks, and wild; but people can be born, and married, and buried in such nooks, and can live, and love, and be loved there as elsewhere, thank God!" The village is portrayed as consisting of "black, coarse-stoned, rough-windowed houses, some with outer staircases, like Swiss houses, a sinuous and stony gutter winding up hill and round the corner by way of street."* The ascent of the mountain was safely achieved, but during the descent Collins unfortunately fell into a watercourse

* "The Lazy Tour of Two Idle Apprentices."

and sprained his ankle, an accident which proved to
be a serious hindrance. They slept that night at
Wigton, which (we are told) " had no population,
no business, no streets to speak of." In *Household
Words* may be found an elaborate, amusing (but
doubtless accurate) description of Wigton market-
place as seen at night nearly fifty years ago, and
written with Dickens's customary power, illustrating
his marvellous acuteness of observation :

" Wigton market was over, and its bare booths
were smoking with rain all down the street. . . .
' I see,' said Brother Francis, ' what I hope and
believe to be one of the most dismal places ever seen
by eyes. I see the houses with their roofs of dull
black, their stained fronts, and their dark-rimmed
windows, looking as if they were all in mourning.
As every little puff of wind comes down the street,
I see a perfect train of rain let off along the wooden
stalls in the market-place and exploded against me.
I see a very big gas-lamp in the centre, which I know,
by a secret instinct, will not be lighted to-night. I
see a pump, with a trivet underneath its spout
whereon to stand the vessels that are brought to be
filled with water. I see a man come to the pump,
and he pumps very hard; but no water follows, and
he strolls empty away. . . . I see one, two, three,
four, five linen-drapers' shops in front of me. I see
a linen-draper's shop next door to the right, and
there are five more linen-drapers' shops round the
corner to the left. Eleven homicidal linen-drapers'
shops within a short stone's-throw, each with its hands
at the throats of all the rest ! Over the small first-
floor of one of these linen-drapers' shops appears the
wonderful inscription : *BANK*. . . . I see a sweet-

meat shop, which the proprietor calls a 'Salt Ware-house.' . . . And I see a watchmaker's, with only three great pale watches of a dull metal hanging in his window, each on a separate pane.

" . . . There is nothing more to see, except the curl-paper bill of the theatre . . . and the short, square, chunky omnibus that goes to the railway, and leads too rattling a life over the stones to hold together long. Oh yes! Now I see two men with their hands in their pockets . . . they are looking at nothing very hard, very hard . . . they spit at times, but speak not. I see it growing darker, and I still see them, sole visible population of the place, standing to be rained upon, with their backs towards me, and looking at nothing very hard.

" . . . The murky shadows are gathering fast, and the wings of evening and the wings of coal are folding over Wigton. . . . And now the town goes to sleep, undazzled by the large unlighted lamp in the market-place ; and let no man wake it."*

From Wigton the friends proceeded to Allonby, on the coast of Cumberland, here resolving to begin their writing, to record their impressions while fresh in their minds. They found a comfortable lodging, a " capital little homely inn," the Ship, overlooking the watery expanse, and by a curious coincidence the landlady previously lived at Greta Bridge, Yorkshire, when Dickens went there in quest of the cheap boarding-schools.

The Ship still flourishes as a " family and commercial hotel and posting-house, commanding extensive views of the Solway Firth and the Scottish hills." Dickens thought Allonby the dullest place he ever

* " The Lazy Tour of Two Idle Apprentices."

THE ALBION HOTEL, BROADSTAIRS. (*Page* 189.)

Dickens stayed at this hotel on several occasions, and in 1839 lodged at a house "two doors from the Albion,"

entered, rendered additionally dull by "the monotony of an idle sea," and in sad contrast to the expectations formed of it. "A little place with fifty houses," said Dickens in a letter home, "five bathing-machines, five girls in straw hats, five men in straw hats, and no other company. The little houses are all in half-mourning—yellow stone or white stone, and black ; and it reminds me of what Broadstairs might have been if it had not inherited a cliff, and had been an Irishman."

In the opinion of Mr. Francis Goodchild, Allonby was the most "delightful place ever seen." "It was what you might call a primitive place. Large? No, it was not large. Who ever expected it would be large? Shape? What a question to ask ! No shape. Shops? Yes, of course (quite indignant). How many? Who ever went into a place to count the shops? Ever so many. Six ? Perhaps. A library ? Why, of course (indignant again). Good collection of books? Most likely—couldn't say— had seen nothing in it but a pair of scales. Any reading-room ? Of course there was a reading-room ! Where ? Where ! Why, over there. Where was over there ? Why, *there !* Let Mr. Idle carry his eye to that bit of waste ground above high-water mark, where the rank grass and loose stones were most in a litter, and he could see a sort of a long ruinous brick loft, next door to a ruinous brick out-house, which loft had a ladder outside to get up by. That was the reading-room, and if Mr. Idle didn't like the idea of a weaver's shuttle throbbing under a reading-room, that was his look-out. *He* was not to dictate, Mr. Goodchild supposed (indignant again), to the company " In short, he declared that "if you wanted to be primitive, you could be primitive here, and if you wanted to be idle, you could be idle here," as were the local fishermen, who (apparently) never fished, but " got their living entirely by looking at the ocean." The " public buildings " at Allonby were the two small bridges over the brook " which crawled or stopped between the houses and the sea." As if to make amends for these shortcomings, Nature provided fine sunsets at Allonby, " when the low, flat beach, with its pools of water and its dry patches, changed into long bars of silver and gold in various states of burnishing," " and there were fine views, on fine days, of the Scottish coast."*

From Allonby the two apprentices proceeded to the county town, Carlisle, putting up at " a capital inn," kept by a man named Breach.

Carlisle " looked congenially and delightfully idle. . . . On market morning Carlisle woke up amazingly, and became (to the two idle apprentices) disagreeably and reproachfully busy. There were its cattle-market, its sheep-market, and its pig-market down by the river, with raw-boned and shock-headed Rob Roys hiding their Lowland dresses beneath heavy plaids, prowling in and out among the animals, and flavouring the air with fumes of whisky. There was its corn-market down the main street, with hum of chaffering over open sacks. There was its general market in the street, too, with heather brooms, on which the purple flower still flourished, and heather baskets primitive and fresh to behold. With women trying on clogs and caps at open stalls, and ' Bible stalls ' adjoining. With ' Dr. Mantle's Dispensary for the Cure of all Human Maladies and no charge for

* " The Lazy Tour of Two Idle Apprentices."

LAWN HOUSE, BROADSTAIRS. *(Page* 193.)

Dickens occupied Lawn House in the summer of 1840, and the archway is mentioned in a
letter to his wife dated September 3, 1850.

advice,' and with 'Dr. Mantle's Laboratory of Medical, Chemical, and Botanical Science,' both healing institutions established on one pair of trestles, one board, and one sun-blind. With the renowned phrenologist from London begging to be favoured (at 6d. each) with the company of clients of both sexes, to whom, on examination of their heads, he would make revelations 'enabling him or her to know themselves.' "*
Maryport, a few miles south of Allonby, was also inspected, and is described as " a region which is a bit of waterside Bristol, with a slice of Wapping, a seasoning of Wolverhampton, and a garnish of Portsmouth "—in fact, a kind of topographical salad. To the supposititious query addressed to it by one of the apprentices, " Will *you* come and be idle with me?" busy Maryport metaphorically shakes its head, and sagaciously answers in the negative, for she declares : " I am a great deal too vaporous, and a great deal too rusty, and a great deal too muddy, and a great deal too dirty altogether ; and I have ships to load, and pitch and tar to boil, and iron to hammer, and steam to get up, and smoke to make, and stone to quarry, and fifty other disagreeable things to do, and I can't be idle with you." Thus thrown upon his own resources, this idle apprentice goes " into jagged up-hill and downhill streets, where I am in the pastry-cook's shop at one moment, and next moment in savage fastnesses of moor and morass, beyond the confines of civilization, and I say to those murky and black-dusty streets : ' Will *you* come and be idle with me?' To which they reply : ' No, we can't indeed, for we haven't the spirits, and we are startled by the echo of your feet on the sharp pavement, and we

* " The Lazy Tour of Two Idle Apprentices."

have so many goods in our shop-windows which nobody wants, and we have so much to do for a limited public which never comes to us to be done for, that we are altogether out of sorts, and can't enjoy ourselves with anyone.' So I go to the Post-office and knock at the shutter, and I say to the Postmaster: ' Will *you* come and be idle with me?' This invitation is refused in cynical terms: ' No, I really can't, for I live, as you may see, in such a very little Post-office, and pass my life behind such a very little shutter, that my hand, when I put it out, is as the hand of a giant crammed through the window of a dwarf's house at a fair, and I am a mere Post-office anchorite in a cell made too small for him, and I can't get in, even if I would.' "* Maryport of to-day differs considerably from Maryport of nearly half a century since, and it is doubtful if its inhabitants will recognise the presentment.

Hesket-New-Market, " that rugged old village on the Cumberland Fells," was included in this itinerary of irresponsible travelling, and of the ancient inn where Idle and Goodchild sojourned, and of the contents of their apartments, we have quite a pre-Raphaelite picture:

" The ceiling of the drawing-room was so crossed and recrossed by beams of unequal lengths, radiating from a centre in the corner, that it looked like a broken star-fish. . . . It had a snug fireside, and a couple of well-curtained windows, looking out upon the wild country behind the house. What it most developed was an unexpected taste for little ornaments and nick-nacks, of which it contained a most surprising number. . . . There were books,

* " The Lazy Tour of Two Idle Apprentices."

too, in this room. . . . It was very pleasant to see these things in such a lonesome byplace; so very agreeable to find these evidences of taste, however homely, that went beyond the beautiful cleanliness and trimness of the house; so fanciful to imagine what a wonder the room must be to the little children born in the gloomy village—what grand impressions of it those of them who became wanderers over the earth would carry away; and how, at distant ends of the world, some old voyagers would die, cherishing the belief that the finest apartment known to man was once in the Hesket-New-Market Inn, in rare old Cumberland."* Dickens does not give the name of the inn, but I have ascertained that it was the Queen's Head, and that it is now a dwelling-house, having the curious-timbered ceiling intact, and still retaining its old-fashioned character. An enclosure, fronting the building, has been planted with shrubs by the present occupier, where it used to be paved and open to the street—" a sinuous and stony gutter winding uphill and round the corner," as Dickens termed the roadway through the still quaint and interesting village of Hesket-New-Market.

On September 12, 1857, Dickens announced that he and his companion were on their way to Doncaster, *en route* for London. Breaking the journey at Lancaster, they stopped at another delightful hostelry, the King's Arms in Market Street. "We are in a very remarkable old house here," wrote Dickens to his sister-in-law, "with genuine old rooms and an uncommonly quaint staircase. I have a state bed-room, with two enormous red four-posters in it, each

* "The Lazy Tour of Two Idle Apprentices."

as big as Charley's room at Gad's Hill."*   A more detailed description, however, appears in the printed record, where we read that "the house was a genuine old house of a very quaint description, teeming with old carvings and beams, and panels, and having an excellent old staircase, with a gallery or upper staircase cut off from it by a curious fence-work of old oak, or of the old Honduras mahogany wood. It was, and is, and will be for many a long year to come, a remarkably picturesque house ; and a certain grave mystery lurking in the depth of the old mahogany panels, as if they were so many deep pools of dark water—such, indeed, as they had been much among when they were trees—gave it a very mysterious character after nightfall."†

In "The Lazy Tour" some particulars are given concerning a curious custom at the King's Arms, where they give you bride-cake every day after dinner. This melodramatic love-story is presented in the form of a narrative by one of the half-dozen "noiseless old men in black" who acted as waiters at the inn, whence we learn that the strange custom originated in the traditional murder, by poison, of a young bride in an apartment afterwards known as the Bride's Chamber, the criminal being subsequently hanged at Lancaster Castle. Around

* "The Letters of Charles Dickens." It is now rumoured that, in the thinning-out process adopted by the Wigton magistrates, some of the oldest established licensed houses in the county are threatened with extinction, all of those in Hesket-New-Market being objected to. Happily, the house immortalized by Dickens will escape, being no longer an inn.

† "The Lazy Tour of Two Idle Apprentices." We are told that "a portion of the lazy notes from which these lazy sheets are taken" was written at the King's Arms Hotel.

FORT HOUSE, BROADSTAIRS. (*Page* 194.)

As it was before the recent alterations. The "airy nest" of Dickens, 1850-1851. A portion of "David Copperfield" was written here,

the legend, in which money and pride and greed and cruel revenge play a prominent part, Dickens threw the halo of his wondrous fancy, and so stimulated public interest in the hostelry that visitors thereto were eager to see the alleged haunted chamber with its antique bedstead of black oak, and to taste the bride-cake in memory of the unfortunate young woman.

Externally, the old King's Arms (situated at the corner of Market Street and King's Street) was not of a picturesque character, although a certain quiet dignity was imparted to the stone frontage by the broad windows extending from roof to basement, and by the pillared doorway of the principal entrance. When Mr. Sly left the old place in 1879, it was pulled down, and a kind of commercial hotel erected on the site, which narrowly escaped destruction by fire in 1897. After his day the custom of having bride-cake was discontinued, but it is interesting to know that the famous oak bedstead (upon which Dickens himself slept) is in the safe possession of the Duke of Norfolk, for whom it was purchased at a high price when the old oak fittings, etc., were disposed of about twenty-seven years since. Mr. Sly, who died in 1896, never tired of recalling the visit of Charles Dickens and Wilkie Collins, and the former delighted the worthy landlord by presenting him with a signed portrait of himself, inscribed, " To his good friend Mr. Sly," which is still retained by the family as a cherished memento. Shortly after the publication of "The Lazy Tour" Mr. Sly obtained permission to reprint the descriptive chapter by Dickens, for presentation to his guests ; the pamphlet contained illustrations representing the entrance-hall and staircase, and this prefatory note : " The reader is perhaps aware that Mr. Charles Dickens and his friend Mr. Wilkie Collins, in the year 1857, visited Lancaster, and during their sojourn stopped at Mr. Sly's, King's Arms Hotel. In the October number of *Household Words*, under the title of ' The Lazy Tour of Two Idle Apprentices,' Mr. Dickens presents his readers with a remarkable story of a Bridal Chamber, from whence the following extracts are taken." Mr. J. Ashby-Sterry, writing in 1897, alludes to the King's Arms as " a rare old place, full of antique furniture, curios, and musical bedsteads," and says that its proprietor, Mr. Sly (who died about a year previously), who took the greatest pride in his admirable old inn, liked nothing better than taking an appreciative visitor over the place and giving amusing reminiscences of the memorable visit of the authors of " Pickwick" and " The Woman in White."

With regard to Lancaster itself, it would seem that Dickens's opinion (as expressed by Francis Goodchild) then was " that if a visitor on his arrival (there) could be accommodated with a pole which could push the opposite side of the street some yards farther off, it would be better for all parties"; but, while " protesting against being obliged to live in a trench," he conceded Lancaster to be a pleasant place—" a place dropped in the midst of a charming landscape, a place with a fine ancient fragment of castle, a place of lovely walks, a place possessing staid old houses richly fitted with old Honduras mahogany, which had grown so dark with time that it seems to have got something of a retrospective mirror-quality into itself, and to show the visitor, in

3 ALBION VILLAS, FOLKESTONE. *(Page* 199.)

"A very pleasant house, overlooking the sea." The opening chapters of "Little Dorrit"
were written here. The conservatory is a modern addition.

THE WOODEN LIGHTHOUSE, FOLKESTONE HARBOUR. *(Page* 200.)

"I may observe of the very little wooden lighthouse, that when it is lighted at night—red and
green—it looks like a medical man's" ("Out of Town").

the depths of its grain, through all its polish, the
hue of the wretched slaves who groaned long ago
under old Lancaster merchants. And Mr. Goodchild adds that the stones of Lancaster do sometimes
whisper even yet of rich men passed away—upon
whose great prosperity some of these old doorways
frowned sullen in the brightest weather—that their
slave-gain turned to curses, as the Arabian Wizard's
money turned to leaves, and that no good ever came
of it even unto the third and fourth generation, until
it was wasted and gone."* Concerning the lunatic
asylum at Lancaster there is a note of approval :
"An immense place . . . admirable offices, very
good arrangements, very good attendants," followed
by this truly Dickensian touch of sympathy and
pathos : " Long groves of blighted men-and-women
trees ; interminable avenues of hopeless faces ;
numbers without the slightest power of really
combining for any earthly purpose ; a society of
human creatures who have nothing in common but
that they have all lost the power of being humanly
social with one another."†

From Lancaster Francis Goodchild and Thomas
Idle took train to Leeds, " of which enterprising
and important commercial centre it may be observed
with delicacy that you must either like it very much
or not at all." Next day, the first of the Race
Week, they proceed to Doncaster, and put up at that
noted establishment the Angel, still flourishing in
the principal thoroughfare as of yore. Here they
had " very good, clean, and quiet apartments " on
the second floor, looking down into the main street,

* " The Lazy Tour of Two Idle Apprentices."
† *Ibid.*

Dickens describing his own bedroom as "airy and clean, little dressing-room attached, eight water-jugs (I never saw such a supply), capital sponge-bath, perfect arrangement, and exquisite neatness."* That great annual festival known as Race Week had just begun, and the streets of Doncaster were full of jockeys, betting men, drunkards, and other undesirable persons, from morning to night—and all night. From their windows the apprentices gazed with interest and wonderment upon the motley assemblage, for this was their first experience of the St. Leger and its saturnalia.

We are assured by Forster that the description here given in "The Lazy Tour" of Doncaster and the races emanated from the pen of Wilkie Collins; I venture, however, to believe that Dickens is more likely to have composed the chapter in question, for not only is it written in his characteristic vein, but we find that when at Doncaster Thomas Idle (*i.e.*, Collins) continued to suffer severely from the accident to his ankle, which practically incapacitated him, and evidently prevented him from witnessing the races. In a letter written at this time Dickens remarks: "I am not going to the course this morning, but have engaged a carriage (open, and pair) for to-morrow and Friday. . . . We breakfast at half-past eight, and fall to work for *H. W.* afterwards. Then I go out, and—hem! look for subjects." The first person singular here is significant, indicating as it does that Collins did not accompany his friend to the scenes so vividly and realistically portrayed in the final chapter of the "Tour." In respect of the visit to Doncaster, a

* "The Letters of Charles Dickens."

THE AULA NOVA AND NORMAN STAIRCASE, PART OF THE KING'S
SCHOOL, CANTERBURY.   (*Page* 203.)

The oldest public school in England, dating from the seventh century, and the original of
Dr. Strong's in "David Copperfield."

HOUSE ON LADY WOOTTON'S GREEN, CANTERBURY.   (*Page* 203.)

Identified as the private residence of Dr. Strong in "David Copperfield."

remarkable incident may be noted. Dickens, who knew nothing (and cared less) about matters relating to the turf, invested in a " c'rect card " containing the names of the horses and jockeys, and, merely for the fun of the thing, wrote down three names for the winners of the three chief races, " and, if you can believe it (he said to Forster) without your hair standing on end, those three races were won, one after another, by those three horses !"* It was the St. Leger Day, which brought ill-fortune to many, so that Dickens's " half-appalling kind of luck " seemed to him especially to be a " wonderful, paralyzing coincidence." He sincerely believed that if a boy with any good in him, but with a damning propensity to sporting and betting, were taken to the Doncaster Races soon enough, it would cure him, so terrible is the revolting exhibition of rascality and the seamy side of humanity.

*   *   *   *   *

Scotland may justly lay claim to an intimate association with Charles Dickens. With the picturesque streets of Edinburgh he first became familiar in 1834, during his reporting days, when he and his colleague, Thomas Beard, represented the *Morning Chronicle* at a grand banquet given at the Scottish capital in honour of the then Prime Minister, Earl Grey, the two young reporters going by sea from London to Leith. This fact explains how Dickens secured such an accurate presentment of the old town of Edinburgh as we find in "Pickwick," in the forty-eighth chapter of which Arthur's Seat is

---

* The successful horses on this day were Impérieuse (St. Leger), Blanche of Middlebec (Municipal Stakes), Skirmisher (Her Majesty's Plate), and Meta (Portland Plate).

described as " towering, surly and dark, like some gruff genius, over the ancient city he has watched so long," while Canongate (as seen by the hero of " The Story of the Bagman's Uncle ") is represented as consisting of " tall, gaunt, straggling houses, with time-stained fronts, and windows that seemed to have shared the lot of eyes in mortals, and to have grown dim and sunken with age. Six, seven, eight stories high were the houses ; story piled above story, as children build with cards, throwing their dark shadows over the roughly-paved road, and making the night darker. A few oil lamps were scattered at long distances, but they only served to mark the dirty entrance to some narrow close, or to show where a common stair communicated, by steep and intricate windings, with the various flats above." We are told that Tom Smart's uncle, on reaching the North Bridge connecting the old town with the new, " stopped for a minute to look at the strange irregular clusters of lights piled one above the other, and twinkling afar off so high that they looked like stars, gleaming from the castle walls on the one side and the Calton Hill on the other, as if they illuminated veritable castles in the air."

The coach-yard (or rather enclosure) in Leith Walk, by which Tom had to pass on the way to his lodging, and where he saw the vision of the old mail-coach with its passengers, actually existed at that spot, and was owned by Mr. Croall, whose family disposed of the carriages and coaches, but subsequently owned all the cabs in the city. Dickens afterwards visited Edinburgh on at least four occasions, staying at the Waterloo Hotel in 1861 and at Kennedy's in 1868, during his Reading tours, and on the latter occasion he observed : " Improvement is beginning to knock the old town of Edinburgh about here and there ; but the Canongate and the most picturesque of the horrible courts and wynds are not to be easily spoiled, or made fit for the poor wretches who people them to live in."* The Scott Monument he could not but regard as a failure, considering that it resembles the spire of a Gothic church taken off and stuck in the ground.

In 1841, on the eve of his departure for the United States, the " Inimitable Boz," accompanied by his wife, made Scotland his destination for a summer holiday tour in " Rob Roy's country," as he termed it. He had thought of Ireland, but altered his mind. The novelist received a magnificent welcome, initiated by a public dinner in Edinburgh, at which Professor Wilson presided. During their brief stay in the Scottish capital Dickens found excellent accommodation at the Royal Hotel, which was consequently besieged, and he was compelled to take refuge in a sequestered apartment at the end of a long passage. His chambers here were "a handsome sitting-room, a spacious bedroom, and large dressing-room adjoining," with another room at his disposal for writing purposes, while from the windows he obtained a noble view, in which the castle formed a conspicuous object. From Edinburgh he travelled to the Highlands, with intervals of rest, and thoroughly admired the characteristic scenery of the country. Especially was he impressed by the Pass of Glencoe, which he had often longed to see, and which he thought " perfectly terrible." " The Pass," he said, " is an awful place. It is shut in on each side

* " The Letters of Charles Dickens."

by enormous rocks, from which great torrents come rushing down in all directions. In amongst these rocks on one side of the Pass . . . there are scores of glens high up, which form such haunts as you might imagine yourself wandering in in the very height and madness of a fever. They will live in my dreams for years. . . . They really are fearful in their grandeur and amazing solitude." Indeed, "that awful Glencoe," as he called it, exercised a kind of fascination over him which proved irresistible, compelling him to revisit the spot the next day, when he found it " absolutely horrific," for " it had rained all night, and . . . through the whole glen, which is ten miles long, torrents were boiling and foaming, and sending up in every direction spray like the smoke of great fires. They were rushing down every hill and mountain side, and tearing like devils across the path, and down into the depths of the rocks. . . . One great torrent came roaring down with a deafening noise and a rushing of water that was quite appalling. . . . The sights and sounds were beyond description." This and other adventures during his journeyings hereabouts were vividly described in letters to Forster, who has printed the major portion of them in his biography, and a very attractive record it is.

Before returning southward, the novelist became the recipient of an invitation to a public dinner at Glasgow ; but, yearning for home, he pleaded pressing business connected with " Master Humphrey's Clock," then appearing in weekly numbers, promising, however, to return a few months later and accept the honour then. Illness unfortunately prevented the fulfilment of that promise, and six years elapsed

THE SUN INN, CANTERBURY. (*Page* 203.)

" It was a little inn where Mr. Micawber put up, and he occupied a little room
in it " (" David Copperfield ").

(1847) before he made acquaintance with that city, when he performed the ceremony of opening the Glasgow Athenæum, which was followed by a soirée in the City Hall. In 1858 he was recommended by some of the students for election as Lord Rector of Glasgow University, in opposition to his own wish, but received only a few votes.

The same year found him again at Edinburgh, and giving, for charitable purposes, a public Reading of the "Carol" in the Music Hall there, at the conclusion of which the Lord Provost presented him with a massive silver wassail-cup, which he bequeathed to his eldest son, and which is now in the possession of Mr. W. H. Lever, of Port Sunlight, Cheshire. His paid Readings subsequently took him to the leading cities in Scotland, and in 1868 he wrote from the Royal Hotel, Glasgow (his customary quarters there) : "The atmosphere of this place, compounded of mists from the Highlands and smoke from the town factories, is crushing my eyebrows as I write, and it rains as it never does rain anywhere else, and always does rain here. It is a dreadful place, though much improved, and possessing a deal of public spirit.*

* "The Letters of Charles Dickens."

CHAPTER VIII.

IN THE MIDLANDS AND HOME COUNTIES.

THE year 1838, in which Charles Dickens, accompanied by "Phiz," hazarded that bitter coach-ride to the northern wilds of Yorkshire, is memorable also for another "bachelor excursion," the two friends travelling by road through the Midlands in the late autumn, *en route* for Warwickshire. They started from the coach office near Hungerford Street, Strand, having booked seats to Leamington, where, on arrival, after a very agreeable (but very cold) journey, they found "a roaring fire, an elegant dinner, a snug room, and capital beds" awaiting them. The "capital inn" affording these creature comforts to the two benumbed passengers was Copps's Royal Hotel, to which reference is made in "Dombey and Son" as the establishment favoured by Mr. Dombey during his stay at Leamington, the scene of his introduction to the lady who became his second wife.

The next morning Dickens and "Phiz" drove in a post-chaise to Kenilworth, "with which we were both enraptured" (the novelist observed in a letter to his wife), and where I really think we *must* have lodgings next summer, please God that we are in good health and all goes well. You cannot conceive

Photochrom Co., Ltd.

GAD'S HILL PLACE. *(Page 205.)*

The home of Charles Dickens from 1857 to 1870.

how delightful it is. To read among the ruins in fine weather would be perfect luxury."* A similar opinion is recorded in his private diary : "Away to Kenilworth — delightful — beautiful beyond expression. Mem. : What a summer resort ! — three months lie about the ruins — books — thinking — seriously turn this over next year." Thence they proceeded to Warwick Castle, to which Dickens referred with less enthusiasm in the same epistle as "an ancient building, newly restored, and possessing no very great attraction beyond a fine view and some beautiful pictures" ; thence to Stratford-on-Avon, where both novelist and artist "sat down in the room where Shakespeare was born, and left our autographs and read those of other people, and so forth." Dickens's entry in the diary recording this circumstance is reminiscent of Alfred Jingle's staccato style ; thus : "Stratford — Shakespeare — the birthplace, visitors, scribblers, old woman—Qy. whether she knows what Shakespeare did, etc." The secretary and librarian of Shakespeare's birthplace (Mr. Richard Savage) informs me that he has understood that these signatures of Dickens and "Phiz" were written upon one of the plaster panels in the birthroom, but have since been destroyed ; the church albums for the years 1848 and 1852 contain signatures of Dickens and of the members of his amateur theatrical company, then touring to raise funds for charitable purposes.†

* "The Letters of Charles Dickens."

† In 1898 the Birthplace Visitors' Books for May, 1821, to September, 1848, in which are preserved the autographs of Sir Walter Scott, Dickens, Washington Irving, and a host of celebrities, were sold at Sotheby's auction-rooms, the four volumes realizing £56.

It is evident that Dickens's first impressions of Stratford were recalled in "Nicholas Nickleby," where Mrs. Nickleby remarks, in her usual inconsequent manner, upon the visit of herself and her husband to the birthplace, and their lodging at a hostelry in the town. Warwick, Kenilworth, and the neighbourhood the author remembered when writing the twenty-seventh chapter of "Dombey and Son," in the description of that "most enchanting expedition" to the castle : "Associations of the Middle Ages, and all that, which is so truly exquisite," exclaimed Cleopatra with rapture ; "such charming times ! So full of faith ! So vigorous and forcible ! So picturesque ! So perfectly removed from the commonplace ! . . . Pictures at the castle, quite divine !" "Those darling bygone times," she observed to Mr. Carker, bent upon showing him the beauties of that historic pile, " with their delicious fortresses, and their dear old dungeons, and their delightful places of torture, and their romantic vengeances, and their picturesque assaults and sieges, and everything that makes life truly charming ! How dreadfully we have degenerated !" Cleopatra and the rest of the little party " made the tour of the pictures, the walls, crow's nest, and so forth," and the castle " being at length pretty well exhausted," and Edith Grainger having completed a sketch of the exterior of the ancient building (concerning which sketch Mr. Carker fawningly avowed that he was unprepared " for anything so beautiful, and so unusual altogether "), a stroll among the haunted ruins of Kenilworth, " and more rides to more points of view . . . brought the day's expedition to a close."

THE LEATHER BOTTLE, COBHAM. (*Page 210.*)

Dickens, in his early days, stayed at the Leather Bottle on more than one occasion, and in 1841 spent a day and

Quitting Stratford the next day, Dickens and his companion intended to proceed to Bridgnorth; but were dismayed to find there were no coaches, which fact compelled them to continue their journey to Shrewsbury and Chester by way of Birmingham and Wolverhampton, "starting by eight o'clock through a cold, wet fog, and travelling, when the day had cleared up, through miles of cinder-paths, and blazing furnaces, and roaring steam-engines, and such a mass of dirt, gloom, and misery, as I never before witnessed."* His impressions of the Black Country are vividly portrayed in the forty-third and succeeding chapters of "The Old Curiosity Shop," and there is good reason to suppose that a portion at least of the itinerary of the pilgrimage of little Nell and her grandfather, after their flight from London to escape from the evil influence of Quilp, was based upon his own tour, undertaken two years previously. Indeed, so far as the above-mentioned chapter is concerned, there is evidence of this in a letter to Forster, apropos of the story, where the novelist says: "You will recognise a description of the road we travelled between Birmingham and Wolverhampton; but I had conceived it so well in my mind that the execution does not please me so well as I expected."

With regard to the depressing effect wrought upon the mind of the traveller through the Black Country, it is gratifying to know that a project is seriously contemplated by which this scene of waste and desolation may be restored to its original condition by reafforestation. Sir Oliver Lodge recently presided at an important meeting held in Birmingham to consider the question, and it was agreed that, now that

* "The Letters of Charles Dickens."

the mineral wealth of the locality had been exhausted, it was only right that the surface of the land should be altered for good by a system of tree-planting, the land itself being rendered useless for mining, agriculture, and habitation.

Birmingham is mentioned frequently throughout the works of Dickens, who visited the city on several occasions, staying at one time at the old Hen and Chickens Inn. He must have known this important manufacturing centre in his journalistic days, for he made it the scene of that well-remembered incident recorded in the fiftieth chapter of " The Pickwick Papers," where Mr. Pickwick calls upon Mr. Winkle, senior, with a difficult and delicate commission. When the post-coach conveying Mr. Pickwick and his friends drew near it was quite dark, " the straggling cottages by the roadside ; the dingy hue of every object visible; the murky atmosphere; the paths of cinders and brick-dust ; the deep red glow of furnace fires in the distance; the volumes of dense smoke issuing heavily forth from high, toppling chimneys, blackening and obscuring everything around ; the glare of distant lights; the ponderous waggons which toiled along the road laden with clashing rods of iron, or piled with heavy goods—all betokened their rapid approach to the great working town of Birmingham. As they rattled through the narrow thoroughfares leading to the heart of the turmoil, the sights and sounds of earnest occupation struck more forcibly on the senses. The streets were thronged with working people. The hum of labour resounded from every house, lights gleamed from the long casement windows in the attic stories, and the whirl of wheels and noise of machinery shook the trembling walls. The fires, whose lurid, sullen light had been visible for miles, blazed fiercely up in the great works and factories of the town. The din of hammers, the rushing of steam, and the dead, heavy clanking of engines, was the harsh music which arose from every quarter." The postboy, driving briskly through the open streets and past the "handsome and well-lighted shops" on the outskirts of the town, drew up at the Old Royal Hotel, where they were shown to a comfortable apartment. The *Old* Royal survives in name only, the present building having been so altered and modernized as to bear no resemblance to the three-storied structure, with its plain, square front and Georgian porch, which temporarily sheltered Mr. Pickwick. The residence of the elder Mr. Winkle ("a wharfinger, Sir, near the canal"), whose name is a familiar one in Birmingham, is believed to be a certain red-brick building in Easy Row, in close proximity to the Old Wharf, a house which, with its white steps leading to the doorway, answers fairly well to the description given in the book.

In 1844 Dickens presided at a meeting of the Polytechnic Institution at Birmingham, and delivered a powerful oration upon the subject of education, comprehensive and unsectarian.

"A better and quicker audience," he afterwards remarked, "never listened to man"; and, in honour of the event, the large hall was profusely decorated with artificial flowers, these also forming the words "Welcome, Boz," in letters about 6 feet high, while about the great organ were immense transparencies bearing designs of an allegorical character. In 1857 he was elected one of the first honorary members of the Birmingham and Midland Institute, in which institution he had always taken an active interest. In January, 1853, at the rooms of the Society of Artists, Temple Row, a large company assembled to witness the presentation to Dickens of a silver-gilt salver and diamond ring, in recognition of valuable services rendered in aid of the fund then being raised for the establishment of the Institute, and as a token of appreciation of his "varied literary acquirements, genial philosophy, and high moral teaching." At the great banquet which followed this interesting function, he offered to give Readings from his books in further aid, and the promise was fulfilled in December, 1853, with the result that nearly £500 were added to the fund; to commemorate these first public Readings, Mrs. Dickens became the recipient of a silver flower-basket.

Other Readings were given in Birmingham in the sixties. In September, 1869, he opened the session of the Midland Institute, the ceremony being rendered memorable by a powerful speech, in which he thus briefly declared his political creed :

"My faith in the people governing is, on the whole, infinitesimal; my faith in the people governed is, on the whole, illimitable." In 1870, as President of the Institute, he distributed at the Town Hall the prizes and certificates awarded to the most successful students; one of the prize-winners was a Miss Winkle, whose name (so reminiscent of "Pickwick") was received with good-humoured laughter, and it is recorded that the novelist, after making some remarks to the lady in an undertone, observed to the audience that he had "recommended Miss Winkle to change her name !"

THE HOUSE AT CHALK IN WHICH DICKENS SPENT HIS HONEYMOON, APRIL, 1836. *(Page* 211.)

Some of the earlier chapters of "Pickwick" were written here.

If a brief note in the diary (under date October 31, 1838) may be accepted as evidence, the travellers stayed at the White Lion in Factory Road, Wolverhampton. Twenty years later (August and November, 1858) Dickens gave public Readings here, and on the first occasion there was a performance of " Oliver Twist " at the local theatre, " in consequence (he opined) of the illustrious author honouring the town with his presence." Writing at this time of the appearance of the country through which he had then passed, he said that it " looked at its blackest " ; " all the furnaces seemed in full blast, and all the coal-pits to be working. . . It is market-day here (Wolverhampton), and the ironmasters are standing out in the street (where they always hold high change), making such an iron hum and buzz that they confuse me horribly. In addition there is a bellman announcing something—not the Readings, I beg to say— and there is an excavation being made in the centre of the open place, for a statue, or a pump, or a lamp-post, or something or other, round which all the Wolverhampton boys are yelling and struggling."*

Reverting to the tour of 1838, Dickens and " Phiz " left Wolverhampton for Shrewsbury (the next stage), making their quarters at the old-fashioned Lion Hotel, which establishment the novelist revisited during the provincial Reading tour of 1858, when he thus described the inn to his elder daughter :

" We have the strangest little rooms (sitting-room and two bedrooms altogether), the ceilings of which I can touch with my hand. The windows bulge out over the street, as if they were little stern

* " The Letters of Charles Dickens "

windows in a ship. And a door opens out of the sitting-room on to a little open gallery with plants in it, where one leans over a queer old rail, and looks all downhill and slantwise at the crookedest black and yellow old houses, all manner of shapes except straight shapes. To get into this room we come through a china closet; and the man in laying the cloth has actually knocked down, in that repository, two geraniums and Napoleon Bonaparte." This quaint establishment, alas! has been modernized (if not entirely rebuilt) since those days, and presents nothing of the picturesqueness that attracted the author of "Pickwick." Shrewsbury, however, still retains and cherishes several of its "black and yellow" (*i.e.*, half-timbered) houses, and it is probably this town which we find thus portrayed in the forty-sixth chapter of "The Old Curiosity Shop": "In the streets were a number of old houses, built of a kind of earth or plaster, crossed and recrossed in a great many directions with black beams, which gave them a remarkable and very ancient look. The doors, too, were arched and low, some with oaken portals and quaint benches, where the former inhabitants had sat on summer evenings. The windows were latticed in little diamond panes, that seemed to wink and blink upon the passengers as if they were dim of sight." On the night of their arrival at Shrewsbury, Dickens and "Phiz" were present at a "bespeak" at the theatre, and witnessed a performance of "The Love Chase," a ballet ("with a phenomenon !"),* followed by divers songs, and the play of "A Roland for an Oliver." "It is a good theatre," was the novelist's comment, "but

* *I.e.*, an infant phenomenon, *à la* Crummles in "Nicholas Nickleby."

THE CORN EXCHANGE, ROCHESTER. (*Page* 214.)

" It is oddly garnished with a queer old clock that projects over the pavement . . . as if
Time carried on business there and hung out his sign " ("Seven Poor Travellers").

the actors are very funny. Browne laughed with such indecent heartiness at one point of the entertainment that an old gentleman in the next box suffered the most violent indignation. The bespeak party occupied two boxes ; the ladies were full-dressed, and the gentlemen, to a man, in white gloves with flowers in their button-holes. It amused us mightily, and was really as like the Miss Snevellicci business as it could well be."*

From the diary we learn that the friends journeyed by post-coach from Shrewsbury over the Welsh border to Llangollen, passing two aqueducts by the way— "beautiful road between the mountains—old abbey at the top of mountain, Denis Brien or Rook Castle — Hand Hotel — Mrs. Phillips — Good." The parish of Llangollen is intersected by the celebrated aqueduct of Pont-y-Lycylltan, and contiguous thereto stands Valle Crucis Abbey. Thence the itinerary included Bangor, Capel Curig, Conway, Chester, Birkenhead, Manchester (Adelphi Hotel), and Cheadle. There is good reason for supposing that Dickens, during this tour, availed himself of the opportunity of visiting the peaceful and picturesque village of Tong, on the north-eastern borders of the county of Salop, and that he probably posted there from Shrewsbury ; for he assured the late Archdeacon Lloyd that Tong Church is the veritable church described in " The Old Curiosity Shop " as the scene of little Nell's death.

" It was a very aged, ghostly place ; the church had been built many hundreds of years ago, and had

---

* " The Letters of Charles Dickens." The reference to " the Miss Snevellicci business " is an allusion to the theatrical incident in " Nicholas Nickleby," chap. xxiv.

once had a convent or monastery attached ; for arches in ruins, remains of oriel windows, and fragments of blackened walls, were yet standing ; while other portions of the old building, which had crumbled away and fallen down, were mingled with the church-yard earth and overgrown with grass, as if they too claimed a burying-place and sought to mix their ashes with the dust of men." Tong Church was erected about the year 1411, and is a fine specimen of Gothic architecture of the Early Perpendicular period. Owing to its fine monuments it is called " The Westminster Abbey of the Midlands." There yet remain the original oak choir-stalls with the miserere seats and carved poppy-heads ; the old oak roof with its sculptured bosses ; the painted screens in the aisles, of very rich workmanship ; and the beautiful Vernon Chantry, called " The Golden Chapel," from its costly ornamentation, referred to in the story as the " baronial chapel." The sacred edifice underwent various reparations during the period between 1810 and 1838, still presenting, however, an exceedingly picturesque aspect when the novelist beheld it in the latter year. Although a more thorough restoration took place in 1892, we are assured that no old features have been destroyed, but doubtless much of the halo of antiquity, which imparts a poetical charm to such structures, is not so evident as of yore. That Dickens derived inspira-tion from Tong and its environment for the "local colouring" in chap. xlvi. and later chapters of " The Old Curiosity Shop " it is impossible to doubt.

In December, 1858, Dickens was entertained at a public dinner at the Castle Hotel, Coventry, on

THE GUILDHALL, ROCHESTER. (*Page* 214.)

Where Pip was bound prentice to Joe Gargery.   Hogarth and his friends played hopscotch
under the colonnade in 1732.

the occasion of receiving a gold repeater watch of special construction by the watchmakers of the town. This gift was tendered as a mark of gratitude for his Reading of the "Christmas Carol," given a year previously in aid of the funds of the Coventry Institute. In acknowledging this testimonial the recipient said :

"This watch, with which you have presented me, shall be my companion in my hours of sedentary working at home and in my wanderings abroad. It shall never be absent from my side, and it shall reckon off the labours of my future days. . . . And when I have done with time and its measurement, this watch shall belong to my children ; and as I have seven boys, and as they have all begun to serve their country in various ways, or to elect into what distant regions they shall roam, it is not only possible, but probable, that this little voice will be heard scores of years hence—who knows?—in some yet unfounded city in the wilds of Australia, or communicating Greenwich time to Coventry Street, Japan. . . . From my heart of hearts I can assure you that the memory of to-night, and of your picturesque and ancient city, will never be absent from my mind, and I can never more hear the lightest mention of the name of Coventry without having inspired in my breast sentiments of unusual emotion and unusual attachment." The novelist bequeathed the watch (and the chain and seals worn with it) to his "dear and trusty friend" John Forster.

In 1849 Dickens was an honoured guest at Rockingham Castle, Northamptonshire, the home of his friends the Hon. Richard Watson and Mrs. Watson.

Writing thence to Forster, he said : " Picture to yourself, my dear F., a large old castle, approached by an ancient keep (gateway), portcullis, etc., filled with company, waited on by six-and-twenty servants. . . and you will have a faint idea of the mansion in which I am at present staying. . . ." His visits to Rockingham were often repeated, and in the winter of 1850 he there supervised the construction of "a very elegant little theatre," of which he constituted himself the manager, and early in the following year the theatre opened with performances of " Used Up," and " Animal Magnetism," with the novelist himself and members of his family in the cast of both plays. Charles Dickens the younger considered that Rockingham Castle bears much more than an accidental resemblance to Chesney Wold, the Lincolnshire mansion of Sir Leicester Dedlock in " Bleak House," upon which story his father was engaged at the period here referred to. Indeed, the author himself confessed as much to Mrs. Watson when he said : " In some of the descriptions of Chesney Wold I have taken many bits, chiefly about trees and shadows, from observations made at Rockingham."

The castle is situated on a breezy eminence overlooking the valley of the Welland, which river overflows occasionally and floods the surrounding country, suggesting the watery Lincolnshire landscape described in the second chapter of " Bleak House." At the end of the terrace is the Yew Walk, corresponding with the Ghost's Walk at Chesney Wold, and there is a sundial in the garden, also referred to in the story. After passing under the archway, flanked by ancient bastion towers (the remains of a former castle), a general view is obtained of the north front of the mansion, one of the principal apartments in which is the long drawing-room, the veritable drawing-room of Chesney Wold, except that the fire-place is surmounted by a carved overmantel instead of a portrait, while the family presentments at Rockingham are in the hall, and not in the drawing-room, as related of those at Chesney Wold. The village of Rockingham consists of one street, which ascends the hill in the direction of the castle lodge; on the right as we enter the village stands "a small inn" called the Sondes Arms, the proto-type of the Dedlock Arms, which bears the date 1763. The "solemn little church" in the park, with its old carved oak pulpit, has been restored and enlarged within the last thirty years. A footpath leading to the church from the village street un-doubtedly answers to Lawrence Boythorn's disputed right-of-way, concerning which that impulsive gentle-man waxes eloquent in the ninth chapter of "Bleak House."

Of the county of Hertford Dickens always re-tained agreeable memories; he frequently followed the advice once offered by him to W. H. Wills, to "take a cheery flutter into the air of Hertfordshire." During the early years of his literary career he indulged a fondness for horse exercise, and, generally accompanied by Forster, would ride to some destina-tion a few miles out of London, take luncheon at some favourite hostelry, and thus enjoy a day's recreation. Their usual refreshment-house on the Great North Road was the Red Lion at High Barnet, in which town Oliver Twist, footsore and weary, found a temporary resting-place on a cold doorstep, and wondered at the great number of taverns there existing, for (as related in the story) "every other house in Barnet was a tavern, large or small." We read in the same story that the infamous Bill Sikes, in his flight after the murder of Nancy, eventually reached Hatfield, turning down "the hill by the church of the quiet village, and, plodding along the little street, crept into a small public-house. . . ." It is evident that Dickens knew Hatfield intimately, the topography of which has since undergone considerable alteration in consequence of the invasion of the Great Northern Railway. The "small public-house" entered by Sikes was in all probability that quaint little ale-house the Eight Bells, still flourishing at the bottom of the main street, while the "little post-office," where he recognised the mail from London, at that time adjoined the Salisbury Arms (now a private residence), at which establishment Dickens himself doubtless stayed on the night of October 27, 1838, when he and "Phiz" made their "bachelor excursion" to the West Country.* Hatfield is introduced in "Mrs. Lirriper's Lodgings,"† for here, in the rural churchyard, Mr. Lirriper was buried; not that Hatfield was his native place (explains the bereaved widow pathetically), "but that he had a liking for the Salisbury Arms, where we went upon our wedding-day, and passed as happy a fortnight as ever happy was." In after-years she "put a sandwich and a drop of sherry in a little basket and went down to Hatfield churchyard, outside the coach, and kissed

* The diary records, under date October 29, 1838: "Hatfield expenses on Saturday, £1 12s."
† Christmas number of *All the Year Round*, 1863.

ROCHESTER ABOUT 1810. (*Page* 215.)

From old prints.

my hand and laid it with a kind of a proud and swelling love on my husband's grave, though, bless you! it had taken me so long to clear his name that my wedding-ring was worn quite fine and smooth when I laid it on the green, green, waving grass."

Mr. Lirriper's youngest brother, by the way, who was something of a scapegrace, also retained a sneaking affection for the Salisbury Arms, derived from less sentimental reasons ; here he enjoyed himself for the space of a fortnight, and left without paying his bill, an omission speedily rectified by the kind-hearted Mrs. Lirriper, in the innocent belief that it was fraternal affection which induced her unprincipled brother-in-law to favour Hatfield with his presence.

In 1859 Dickens became much interested in a working men's club established at Rothamsted by the late Sir John Bennet Lawes, the renowned scientist, the purpose of this club being to enable all agricultural labourers of the parish to enjoy their ale and pipes independently of the public-house. The novelist, accompanied by his brother-in-law, Henry Austin, drove to Rothamsted for the express purpose of inspecting this novel institution, which numbers to-day nearly 200 members, and was so delighted with what he saw and heard respecting it that he not only published an article on the subject,* but eagerly recommended the formation of such clubs in other country neighbourhoods. Sir John Lawes is, of course, the prototype of Friar Bacon in the article aforesaid, where the worthy baronet's beautiful manor-house (in which his son and heir now resides) is thus described : " The sun burst forth

* " The Poor Man and his Beer " in *All the Year Round*, April 30, 1859.

gaily in the afternoon, and gilded the old gables, and old mullioned windows, and old weathercock, and old clock-face, of the quaint old house which is the dwelling of the man we sought. How shall I describe him? As one of the most famous practical chemists of the age? That designation will do as well as another—better, perhaps, than most others. And his name? Friar Bacon. . . . We walked on the trim garden terrace before dinner, among the early leaves and blossoms ; two peacocks, apparently in very tight new boots, occasionally crossing the gravel at a distance. The sun shining through the old house-windows now and then flashed out some brilliant piece of colour from bright hangings within, or upon the old oak panelling ; similarly, Friar Bacon, as we paced to and fro, revealed little glimpses of his good work."

In "Bleak House" Hertfordshire plays a conspicuous part, and it is generally believed that the original of John Jarndyce's residence, which gives its name to the story, is to be discovered in or near St. Albans, as mentioned in the book itself. Indeed, a picturesque Early Georgian building at the top of Gombards Road (on the northern outskirts of the city) has been christened "Bleak House" in the supposition that it was the veritable home of Mr. Jarndyce ; and there appears to be some justification for this, as the position of the house in its relation to the abbey church, and the characteristics of the locality, are in harmony with the details particularized in the story. There is evidence, too, that Dickens lodged in St. Albans when engaged upon the early chapters of his novel ; he and Douglas Jerrold stayed at the Queen's Hotel in Chequer Street, and it was then rumoured in the town that the object of Dickens's visit was to obtain "local colour." His younger brother Frederick and his friend Peter Cunningham lived for a while in St. Albans, and it is remembered by some of the older inhabitants that the author of "Pickwick" occasionally journeyed to St. Albans, when opportunities arose, for a gossip with those boon companions in their country retreat.

Of all Hertfordshire localities with which Dickens formed an acquaintance, that claiming the most intimate association with him is the pretty little village of Knebworth, the ancestral home of the Lyttons. A warm friendship existed between Lord Lytton and his brother novelist, and when, in 1850, some private threatricals were arranged for performance in the grand banqueting-hall, with "Boz" and his goodly company of amateurs in the cast (including Leech, Lemon, Tenniel, Stanfield, Forster, and others), mirth and jollity reigned supreme. The plays went off "in a whirl of triumph" (wrote Dickens at the time), "and fired the whole length and breadth of Hertfordshire," which is not surprising when the circumstances are recalled. At Knebworth originated that unfortunate scheme known as the "Guild of Literature and Art," formulated by Dickens and Lord Lytton for the amelioration of the hardships of impecunious authors and artists, the funds in aid of the project being augmented by the proceeds derived from the theatrical entertainments. It was intended to erect and endow a retreat for such necessitous persons, and a block of houses (in the Gothic style) was actually built upon ground near the main road at Stevenage, given by Lord Lytton for the purpose. Unhappily, these praiseworthy efforts failed to appeal to those for whose benefit they were designed, and the guild houses, after remaining unoccupied for nearly twenty years, were converted into "suburban villas," the rents being available for the relief of such applicants as were qualified to receive it. It was generally believed that the failure to secure tenants for the guild houses under the special regulations was due chiefly to the fact of their being regarded as little better than almshouses, and too remote from London to be easily accessible ; it must not be forgotten, too, that true genius looks askance at acts of charity performed in its behalf, the spirit of independence which usually characterizes it rebelling at anything that appears to assume the form of patronage, although it must be admitted that the guild rules give no cause for suspicion on that score. Dickens, in a speech delivered in 1865, after a survey of the newly-completed and attractive domiciles, said : " The ladies and gentlemen whom we shall invite to occupy the houses we have built will never be placed under any social disadvantage. They will be invited to occupy them as artists, receiving them as a mark of the high respect in which they are held by their fellow-workers. As artists, I hope they will often exercise their calling within those walls for the general advantage ; and they will always claim, on equal terms, the hospitality of their generous neighbour." But it was not to be, and probably nothing proved so disappointing to Dickens as the almost contemptuous indifference with which this philanthropic proposal was received both by the press and the public, who ridiculed it unmercifully. As a memento of the scheme, there may be seen nearly opposite the guild houses a roadside tavern rejoicing in the sign of Our Mutual Friend, intended as a delicate compliment to the author of the story so entitled, then in course of publication.

During a visit to Knebworth in 1861, Dickens and Mr. (afterwards Sir) Arthur Helps—sometime Queen's Secretary—called upon a most extraordinary character, locally known as " Mad Lucas," who lived in an extremely miserly fashion in the kitchen of his house (Elmwood House, at Redcoats Green, near Stevenage). This strange recluse died of apoplexy in 1874, and was buried in Hackney Churchyard ; his house, with its boarded-up windows, shored-up walls, and dilapidated roof, continued to remain an object of interest for many years afterwards, until in 1893 it was razed to the ground and the materials sold by public auction. James Lucas, "the Hertfordshire Hermit," was really a well-educated and highly intellectual man, who inherited the estate of his father, a prosperous West India merchant, and it is conjectured that his distress at the death of his widowed mother (who lived with him) was primarily the cause of that mental aberration which assumed such an eccentric form ; he even refused to bury her corpse, so that the local authorities were compelled to resort to a subterfuge in order to perform themselves the last rites. He objected to furnish his rooms, and, attired simply in a loose blanket fastened with a skewer, preferred to eat and sleep amidst the cinders and rubbish-heaps (a sanctuary for rats) which accumulated in the kitchen. Although his diet consisted of bread and cheese, red herrings, and gin, there were choice wines available for friendly visitors, a special vintage of sherry being reserved for ladies who thus honoured him. The hermit's penchant for tramps attracted all the vagabonds in the neighbourhood, so that it became necessary for him to protect himself from insult by retaining armed watchmen and barricading the house.

In "Tom Tiddler's Ground"* Dickens has depicted a miserly recluse named Mopes, and it is easy to discern that Lucas sat for the portrait— indeed, it is said that in reading the number he recognised the presentment, and expressed great indignation at what he considered to be a much exaggerated account of himself and his environment. In the chapter devoted to Mr. Mopes, the novelist tells us that he found his strange abode in "a nook in a rustic by-road, down among the pleasant dales and trout-streams of a green English county." He does not think it necessary for the reader to know what county; suffice it to say that one "may hunt there, shoot there, fish there, traverse long grass-grown Roman roads there, open ancient barrows there, see many a mile of richly-cultivated land there, and hold Arcadian talk with a bold peasantry, their country's pride, who will tell you (if you want to know) how pastoral housekeeping is done on nine shillings a week."

Those familiar with this portion of Hertfordshire cannot fail to recognise in these allusions the neighbourhood of Stevenage, and a clue to its identity is afforded by the allusion to "ancient barrows," for at Stevenage there are some remarkable tumuli known as the "Six Hills," which are believed to be ancient sepulchral barrows, or repositories of the dead. If further evidence be required, it is forthcoming in the

* The Christmas number of *All the Year Round*, 1861.

following delightful portrayal of Stevenage itself, as it appeared to Dickens over forty years ago :

"The morning sun was hot and bright upon the village street. The village street was like most other village streets: wide for its height, silent for its size, and drowsy in the dullest degree. The quietest little dwellings with the largest of window-shutters (to shut up Nothing as carefully as if it were the Mint or the Bank of England) had called in the Doctor's house so suddenly that his brass doorplate and three stories stood among them as conspicuous and different as the Doctor himself in his broadcloth among the smock frocks of his patients. The village residences seem to have gone to law with a similar absence of consideration, for a score of weak little lath-and-plaster cabins clung in confusion about the Attorney's red-brick house, which, with glaring door-steps and a most terrific scraper, seemed to serve all manner of ejectments upon them. They were as various as labourers—high-shouldered, wry-necked, one-eyed, goggle-eyed, squinting, bow-legged, knock-kneed, rheumatic, crazy ; some of the small trades-men's houses, such as the crockery shop and the harness-maker's, had a Cyclops window in the middle of the gable, within an inch or two of its apex, suggesting that some forlorn rural Prentice must wriggle himself into that apartment horizontally, when he retired to rest, after the manner of the worm. So bountiful in its abundance was the sur-rounding country, and so lean and scant the village, that one might have thought the village had sown and planted everything it once possessed to convert the same into crops. This would account for the bareness of the little shops, the bareness of the few boards and trestles designed for market purposes in a corner of the street, the bareness of the obsolete inn and inn yard, with the ominous inscription, 'Excise Office,' not yet faded out from the gateway, as indicating the very last thing that poverty could get rid of. . . ." The village alehouse, mentioned in the first chapter of "Tom Tiddler's Ground," and there called the Peal of Bells, is the White Hart, Stevenage, where Dickens called on his way to see Lucas to inquire of the landlord, old Sam Cooper, the shortest route to the "ruined hermitage of Mr. Mopes the hermit," some five miles distant. He found Tom Tiddler's Ground to be "a nook in a rustic by-road, which the genius of Mopes had laid waste as completely as if he had been born an Emperor and a Conqueror. Its centre object was a dwelling-house, sufficiently substantial, all the window-glass of which had been long ago abolished by the surprising genius of Mopes, and all the windows of which were barred across with rough-split logs of trees nailed over them on the outside. A rick-yard, hip high in vegetable rankness and ruin, contained out-buildings, from which the thatch had lightly fluttered away . . . and from which the planks and beams had heavily dropped and rotted." After noting the fragments of mildewed ricks and the slimy pond, the traveller encountered the hermit himself, as well as he could be observed between the window-bars, "lying on a bank of soot and cinders, on the floor, in front of a rusty fireplace," when presently began the interview with "the sooty object in blanket and skewer," as related in the narrative with approximate exactitude.

CHAPTER IX.

IN DICKENS LAND.

"KENT, sir! Everybody knows Kent. Apples, cherries, hops, and women." Thus did Alfred Jingle briefly summarize for the behoof of Tracy Tupman the principal characteristics of the county which, by general consent, is termed "the Garden of England," a designation richly merited through its sylvan charms and other natural beauties.

This division of south-eastern England is rightly considered as the very heart of Dickens land, for the reason that no other locality (excepting, of course, the great Metropolis) possesses such numerous associations with the novelist and his writings. He himself practically admitted as much when, in 1840, he said: "I have many happy recollections connected with Kent, and am scarcely less interested in it than if I had been a Kentish man bred and born, and had resided in the county all my life." It was in Kent, too, where he made his last home and where he drew his last breath.

As already narrated in the opening chapter of this volume, some of Dickens's earliest years were spent at Chatham, and the locality within the radius of a few miles became familiar to him by means of pedestrian excursions with his father; indeed, it was during one of these delightful jaunts that he first saw the house at Gad's Hill which subsequently became his own property, and the incident is thus faithfully recorded (although thinly disguised) in one of "The Uncommercial Traveller" papers :

" So smooth was the old highroad, and so fresh were the horses, and so fast went I, that it was midway between Gravesend and Rochester, and the widening river was bearing the ships, white-sailed or black-smoked, out to sea, when I noticed by the wayside a very queer small boy.

"'Halloa !' said I to the very queer small boy. 'Where do you live ?'

"'At Chatham,' says he.

"'What do you do there ?' says I.

"'I go to school,' says he.

" I took him up in a moment, and we went on. Presently the very queer small boy says : 'This is Gad's Hill we are coming to, where Falstaff went out to rob those travellers, and ran away.'

"'You know something about Falstaff, eh ?' said I.

"'All about him,' said the very queer small boy. 'I am old (I am nine), and I read all sorts of books. But *do* let us stop at the top of the hill, and look at the house there, if you please.'

"'You admire that house ?' said I.

"'Bless you, sir !' said the very queer small boy, 'when I was not more than half as old as nine it used to be a treat for me to be brought to look at it. And ever since I can recollect my father, seeing me so fond of it, has often said to me : "If you were to be very persevering, and were to work hard, you might some day come to live in it," though that's impossible,' said the very queer small boy, drawing a low breath, and now staring at the house out of the window with all his might.

"I was rather amazed to be told this by the very queer small boy, for that house happens to be *my* house, and I have reason to believe that what he said was true."*

In another "Uncommercial" paper Dickens recorded his impressions of a later visit to this neighbourhood: "I will call my boyhood's home . . . Dullborough," he says, and further observes that he found himself rambling about the scenes among which his earliest days were passed—"scenes from which I departed when a child, and which I did not revisit until I was a man," when he found the place strangely altered, for the railway had since disfigured the land. The railway-station "had swallowed up the playing-field, the two beautiful hawthorn-trees, the hedge, the turf, and all those buttercups and daisies had given place to the stoniest of roads; while, beyond the station, an ugly dark monster of a tunnel kept its jaws open, as if it had swallowed them and were ravenous for more destruction." He confesses that he was not made happy by the disappearance of the old familiar landmarks of his boyhood, but adds reflectively: "Who was I that I should quarrel with the town for being so changed to me, when I myself had come back, so changed, to it? All my early readings and early imaginations dated from this place, and I took them away so full of innocent construction and guileless belief, and I brought them back so worn and torn, so much the wiser and so much the worse."

In the same paper reference is made to the Dull-

* "Travelling Abroad."

borough (*i.e.*, Chatham) Mechanics' Institute—"There had been no such thing in the town in my young days"—which he found with some difficulty, for the reason that "it led a modest and retired existence up a stable-yard." He learned, however, that it was "a most flourishing institution, and of the highest benefit to the town, two triumphs which I was glad to understand were not at all impaired by the seeming drawbacks that no mechanics belonged to it, and that it was steeped in debt to the chimney-pots. It had a large room, which was approached by an infirm stepladder, the builder having declined to construct the intended staircase without a present payment in cash, which Dullborough (though profoundly appreciative of the Institution) seemed unaccountably bashful about subscribing." In aid of the funds Dickens soon afterwards gave some public Readings in this very building, with the result that its financial position was considerably improved.

Dickens's affection for Kent is indicated by the fact that he selected that county in which to spend his honeymoon, and in the village of Chalk (near Gravesend, on the main road to Dover) may still be seen the cottage where that happy period was spent, and in which he wrote some of the earlier pages of "Pickwick."* It is a corner house on the southern side of the road, advantageously situated for commanding views of the river Thames and the far-stretching landscape beyond. In after-years, whenever his walks led him to this spot, he invariably slackened his pace on arriving at the house, and

* Probably that portion descriptive of Cobham village and park was penned here. His landlord, Thomas White, was still living in 1883.

meditatively glanced at it for a few moments, mentally reviving the time when he and his bride found a pleasant home within its hospitable walls. Shortly after the birth of their eldest son, Dickens and his wife stayed at the honeymoon cottage, which, with its red-tiled roof and dormer windows, is a picturesque object on this famous coaching road. The walk to Chalk Church was much favoured by the novelist, where a quaint carved figure over the entrance porch interested him. This curious piece of sculpture, which he always greeted with a friendly nod, is supposed to represent an old priest grasping by the neck a large urn-like vessel, concerning which there is probably a legend. Another grotesque is seen above, and between the two is a niche, in which formerly stood an image of the virgin saint (St. Mary) to whom this thirteenth-century church is dedicated. About a mile distant, and a little south of the main road, is Shorne, another typical Kentish village, which, with its church and burial-ground, constituted for Dickens another source of attraction, and the latter was probably in his mind when he referred (in " Pickwick ") to " one of the most peaceful and secluded churchyards in Kent, where wild-flowers mingle with the grass, and the soft landscape around forms the fairest spot in the garden of England." Shorne formerly boasted a celebrity, one Sir John Shorne, who achieved fame by the curing of ague and gained notoriety as the custodian of the devil, whom, it is alleged, he imprisoned in a boot, with the result that shrines were erected to his memory.*

Of the towns in Southern England associated with Dickens, perhaps none is more replete with memories

---

* Miller's "Jottings of Kent," 1871.

of the novelist than Broadstairs. It was but a little
Kentish watering-place when, in the autumn of 1837,
he and his wife first passed a seaside holiday there, at
No. 12 (now No. 31), High Street, a humble-look-
ing tenement of two storeys in height, with a small
parlour facing the narrow thoroughfare ; the house
survived until a few years ago, although in an altered
form, and has since been rebuilt. In 1890 it was
tenanted by a plumber and glazier, who apparently
did not know of its literary associations, for here
were written some of the later pages of " Pickwick."
Formerly of some importance, Broadstairs at this
time had just emerged from the condition of a village
into which it had lapsed, and in 1842 began to attain
some celebrity as a place of fashionable resort for
sea-bathing. Dickens delighted in the quietude of
the spot, and Broadstairs became his favourite summer
or autumn resort for many years. In 1839 we find
him located at No. 40, Albion Street (two doors
from the Albion Hotel), where he finished the
writing of " Nicholas Nickleby," and composed the
dedication of that story to his cherished friend
Macready. During the following year he went twice
to Broadstairs, being then at work upon "The Old
Curiosity Shop," and in all probability found a lodgment in the Albion Street house ; for, writing to
Maclise the day after his arrival there, on June 1,
he urged him to "come to the bower which is shaded
for you in the one-pair front, where no chair or table
has four legs of the same length, and where no
drawers will open till you have pulled the pegs off,
and then they keep open and won't shut again."
In 1845 he and his family engaged rooms for the
month of August at the Albion Hotel, and again,

apparently, in 1847, judging from an allusion to his
" looking out upon a dark gray sea, with a keen
north-east wind blowing it in shore."   The Albion
was favoured by him in 1859,* when, suffering in
health, he went for a week's sea air and change, to
prepare himself for the exacting labours of a provincial Reading tour.   Dickens delighted to entertain
his friends at the Albion, where, upon one of the
walls, hangs an original letter containing a description
of Broadstairs, penned by the novelist himself :

" A good sea—fresh breezes—fine sands—and
pleasant walks—with all manner of fishing-boats,
lighthouses, piers, bathing-machines, are its only
attractions ; but it is one of the freshest and freest
little places in the world."   Here, too, is jealously
preserved an ancient oak chest on which he was wont
to sit while he and his intimates quaffed the old
hostelry's unrivalled milk-punch.

An amusing description of his mode of life at
Broadstairs—of the mild distractions and innocent
pleasures to be enjoyed there—is discoverable in a
characteristic letter addressed by him to Professor
Felton from that watering-place in 1843 : " This is
a little fishing-place ; intensely quiet ; built on a
cliff, whereon, in the centre of a tiny semicircular
bay, our house stands, the sea rolling and dashing
under the windows.   Seven miles out are the Goodwin Sands (you've heard of the Goodwin Sands ?),
whence floating lights perpetually wink after dark,
as if they were carrying on intrigues with the servants.
Also there is a big lighthouse called the North

---

* It would seem, from the published correspondence of 1859,
that the house (No. 40, Albion Street) occupied by him twenty
years previously had been absorbed by the hotel.

Foreland on a hill behind the village—a severe, parsonic light, which reproves the young and giddy floaters, and stares grimly out upon the sea. Under the cliff are rare good sands, where all the children assemble every morning and throw up impossible fortifications, which the sea throws down again at high-water. Old gentlemen and ancient ladies flirt after their own manner in two reading-rooms and on a great many scattered seats in the open air. Other old gentlemen look all day through telescopes and never see anything. In a bay-window in a one-pair sits, from nine o'clock to one, a gentleman with rather long hair and no neckcloth, who writes and grins as if he thought he were very funny indeed. His name is Boz. At one he disappears, and presently emerges from a bathing-machine, and may be seen—a kind of salmon-coloured porpoise—splashing about in the ocean. After that he may be seen in another bay-window on the ground-floor eating a strong lunch ; after that walking a dozen miles or so, or lying on his back in the sand reading a book. Nobody bothers him unless they know he is disposed to be talked to, and I am told he is very comfortable indeed. He's as brown as a berry, and they *do* say is a small fortune to the innkeeper, who sells beer and cold punch. But this is mere rumour. Sometimes he goes up to London (eighty miles or so away), and then, I'm told, there is a sound in Lincoln's Inn Fields (Forster's residence) at night as of men laughing, together with a clinking of knives and forks and wineglasses."* Again, in 1850 : "You will find it the healthiest and freshest of places, and there are Canterbury, and all varieties of what Leigh

* " The Letters of Charles Dickens."

Hunt calls 'greenery,' within a few minutes' railroad ride. It is not very picturesque ashore, but extremely so seaward, all manner of ships continually passing close inshore." Writing to the Earl of Carlisle in 1851, he jocularly said : " The general character of Broadstairs as to size and accommodation was happily expressed by Miss Eden, when she wrote to the Duke of Devonshire (as he told me), saying how grateful she felt to a certain sailor, who asked leave to see her garden, for not plucking it bodily up and sticking it in his buttonhole. You will have for a night-light," he added, " in the room we shall give you, the North Foreland lighthouse. That and the sea and air are our only lions. It is a rough little place, but a very pleasant one, and you will make it pleasanter than ever to me."* To Forster at this time he remarked of his Broadstairs environment: " It is more delightful here than I can express. Corn growing, larks singing, garden full of flowers, fresh air on the sea—oh, it is wonderful !" One of his minor writings is wholly devoted to a description of " Our Watering-Place " (for so the paper is entitled), in which there are many happy touches recalling Broadstairs of more than fifty years ago. Here is the beach as seen at low tide: " The ocean lies winking in the sunlight like a drowsy lion ; its glassy waters scarcely curve upon the shore ; the fishing-boats in the tiny harbour are all stranded in the mud. Our two colliers . . . have not an inch of water within a quarter of a mile of them, and turn exhausted on their sides, like faint fish of an antediluvian species. Rusty cables and chains, ropes and rings, undermost parts of posts and piles,

* " The Letters of Charles Dickens."

and confused timber defences against the waves, lie
strewn about in a brown litter of tangled seaweed
and fallen cliff. . . . The time when this pretty
little semicircular sweep of houses, tapering off at the
end of the wooden pier into a point in the sea, was a
gay place, and when the lighthouse overlooking
it shone at daybreak on company dispersing from
public balls, is but dimly traditional now." The
following depicts, with the skill of a master hand,
the same scene at high-water : " The tide has risen ;
the boats are dancing on the bubbling water ; the
colliers are afloat again ; the white-bordered waves
rush in. . . . The radiant sails are gliding past the
shore and shining on the far horizon ; all the sea is
sparkling, heaving, swelling up with life and beauty
this bright morning." To the parish church the
author refers disrespectfully as "a hideous temple of
flint, like a great petrified haystack," and of the pier,
built in 1809, he says : " We have a pier—a queer
old wooden pier, fortunately—without the slightest
pretensions to architecture, and very picturesque in
consequence. Boats are hauled up upon it, ropes are
coiled all over it ; lobster-pots, nets, masts, oars, spars,
sails, ballast, and rickety capstans, make a perfect
labyrinth of it." In the same paper he observes :
" You would hardly guess which is the main street
of our watering-place,* but you may know it by
its being always stopped up with donkey-chaises.
Whenever you come here, and see harnessed donkeys
eating clover out of barrows drawn completely across
a narrow thoroughfare, you may be quite sure you

* " Our Watering-Place," first published in *Household Words*
August 2, 1851, was reprinted as " Our English Watering-
Place."

are in our High Street."* The reference here to donkeys prompts the statement that at Broadstairs lived the original of Betsy Trotwood in "David Copperfield." She was a Miss Strong, who occupied a double-fronted cottage in the middle of Nuckell's Place, on the sea-front, and who, like the admirable Betsy, was firmly convinced of her right to stop the passage of donkeys along the road opposite her door, deterring their proprietors by means of hostile demonstrations with a hearth-broom. Close by there is a cottage which has been christened Dickens House, and in Broadstairs there is a Dickens Road.

Tired of the discomforts of seaside lodgings, Dickens began to search for a house at Broadstairs which he could hire for the period of his annual visits. He discovered in Fort House a residence that seemed to fulfil his requirements ; but it was not yet available, and he was fain to content himself for a while with Lawn House, a smaller villa, the garden of which adjoins the western boundary of the grounds of Fort House. Abutting upon the south side of Lawn House, whence a good view of the German Ocean is obtainable, is the archway referred to in one of the published letters,† spanning the narrow road approached from Harbour Street and leading to the coastguard station, this road passing the front of Fort House between it and the sea-wall. Not until the autumn of 1850 did he succeed in obtaining possession of Fort House, situated on the Kingsgate Road, perched upon the summit of a bold headland of the Thanet cliffs, with a superb panorama of sea

* See the letter to Mrs. Charles Dickens, September 3, 1850.
† *Ibid.*

and country. At that time there was a cornfield between the house and the harbour. Alas! a cornfield no longer, but land upon which some cottages and stables have since been built, these partly obstructing the view southward.

Fort House, to which were attached pleasure grounds of about an acre in extent, was approached by a carriage drive, and the rental value in 1883 was £100 a year. This "airy nest" (as he described his Broadstairs home) formed a conspicuous landmark in the locality, and proved a constant source of attraction to visitors by reason of its associations. Edmund Yates thus describes it as seen by him at a subsequent period: " It is a small house without any large rooms, but such a place as a man of moderate means, with an immoderate family of small children, might choose for a summer retreat. The sands immediately below afford a splendid playground ; there is an abundant supply of never-failing ozone ; there is a good lawn, surrounded by borders well-stocked with delicious-smelling common English flowers, and there is, or was in those days, I imagine, ample opportunity for necessary seclusion. The room in which Dickens worked is on the first floor, a small, three-cornered slip, ' about the size of a warm bath,' as he would have said, but with a large expansive window commanding a magnificent sea-view. His love for the place, and his gratitude for the good it always did him, are recorded in a hundred letters." In 1889 the late Mr. W. R. Hughes and the present writer were privileged to examine Fort House, and our impressions have been duly recorded. We approached the study by a little staircase leading from the first floor, and from the veranda-shaded

window witnessed a lovely view of the sea.   Perhaps
it was nothing more than coincidence, but Dickens
seemed to prefer, as places of residence, houses having
semicircular frontages, and Fort House proved no
exception, his study being in the bowed front facing
the ocean.   Here he wrote the concluding lines of
what the author himself regarded as the best of all
his books, " David Copperfield."   Let it be distinctly averred that not a line of " Bleak House "
was penned in this abode (as is generally supposed),
and that it is quite an erroneous idea to associate
Fort House with the home of Mr. Jarndyce, so
minutely described in that story.   This being the
case, it is unfortunate that a later owner of the
property committed the indiscretion of changing the
name of the building to Bleak House, by which
misleading designation it has been known for a considerable period.

After a good many years of disuse, Bleak House
fell into a lamentable state of decay, and it is much
to be deplored that the local authorities did not avail
themselves of the opportunity afforded them of
acquiring (for the sake of preservation) the residence
which so frequently became the favourite seaside
dwelling of the genius of the place.   They, however,
did not rise to the occasion, with the result that, in
consequence of remaining so long uninhabited, the
house suffered seriously from dilapidation, and the
garden (containing the old swing where the novelist
used to swing his children) became a wilderness of
weeds.   Recently the property was sold, and the
owner thought fit to restore, alter, and extend the
premises, converting the building into a pretentious-
looking mansion of Tudor design, with castellated

eaves and other "improvements," by which it is changed beyond all recognition.

In 1847 Broadstairs commenced to grow out of favour with the novelist, for it then began to attract large numbers of holiday folks, with an attendant train of outdoor entertainers, who deprived him of that quietude and seclusion so indispensable for his work.   "Vagrant music is getting to that height here," he said, "and is so impossible to be escaped from, that I fear Broadstairs and I must part company in time to come.   Unless it pours of rain, I cannot write half an hour without the most excruciating organs, fiddles, bells, or glee-singers.   There is a violin of the most torturing kind under the window now (time, ten in the morning), and an Italian box of music on the steps, both in full blast."   Dickens did not desert the town just yet, however, as in 1851 (in order to escape the excitement in London caused by the Great Exhibition) he decided to let the town house (Devonshire Terrace) for a few months, and engaged Fort House from the beginning of May until November, his longest sojourn at Broadstairs. This was not the last visit (as stated in a note in the published " Letters "), as he spent a week there in the summer of 1859 for sea air and change, thus to assist recovery from a slight illness, and prepare for the severe ordeal of a provincial Reading tour.   After 1859 Broadstairs knew him no more, although we are assured that he ever retained an affectionate interest in that " pretty little watering-place."   Mr. Hughes has recorded an interview with an " old salt," one Harry Ford, who well remembered the novelist when, in early days, he (Dickens) went with his family to stay at Broadstairs.   " Bless your soul !"

he said, "I can see 'Old Charley' (as we used to call him among ourselves here) a-coming flying down from the cliff with a hop, step, and jump, with his hair all flying about. He used to sit sometimes on that rail"—pointing to the one surrounding the harbour—"with his legs lolling about, and sometimes on the seat that you're a-sitting on now" (adjoining the old look-out house opposite the Tartar Frigate Inn), "and he was very fond of talking to us fellows and hearing our tales; he was very good-natured, and nobody was liked better. And if you'll read that story that he wrote and printed about 'Our Watering-Place,' *I* was the man who's mentioned there as mending a little ship for a boy. *I* held that child between my knees. And, what's more, *I* took 'Old Charley,' on the very last time that he came over to Broadstairs (he wasn't living here at the time), round the Foreland to Margate, with a party of four friends. I took 'em in my boat, the *Irene*"—pointing to a clinker-built, strong boat lying in the harbour, capable of holding twenty people. "The wind was easterly, the weather was rather rough, and it took me three or four hours to get round. There was a good deal of chaffing going on, I can tell you."*

Of the neighbouring watering-place, Margate, but little can be said from the Dickensian point of view, for the novelist visited it so seldom, probably not more than twice—viz., in 1844 and 1847, writing thence on both occasions to Forster with particular reference to the theatre there, which he honoured with his patronage. In this respect Dover comes within the same category, for he said, in 1852: "It

* "A Week's Tramp in Dickens Land," by W. R. Hughes, F.L.S.

is not quite a place to my taste, being too bandy (I mean musical; no reference to its legs), and infinitely too genteel. But the sea is very fine, and the walks are quite remarkable. There are two ways of going to Folkestone, both lovely and striking in the highest degree, and there are heights and downs and country roads, and I don't know what, everywhere." Mention is frequently made of Dover in his books— of its castle, pier, cliffs, harbour, theatre, etc.; the latter, built in 1790, he described in 1856 as "a miserable spectacle—the pit is boarded over, and it is a drinking and smoking place." Here is a pen-picture of the fortified town from "A Tale of Two Cities," as it appeared more than a century ago : "The little narrow, crooked town of Dover hid itself away from the beach, and ran its head into the chalk cliffs, like a marine ostrich. The beach was a desert of heaps of sea and stones tumbling wildly about, and the sea did what it liked, and what it liked was destruction. It thundered at the town, and thundered at the cliffs, and brought the coast down, madly. The air among the houses was of so strong a piscatory flavour that one might have supposed sick fish went up to be dipped in it, as sick people went down to be dipped in the sea. A little fishing was done in the port, and a quantity of strolling about by night, and looking seaward, particularly at those times when the tide made, and was near flood. Small tradesmen, who did no business whatever, sometimes unaccountably realized large fortunes, and it was remarkable that nobody in the neighbourhood could endure a lamplighter." In "The Uncommercial Traveller," too, we find this pleasing fancy in alluding to Dover : "There the sea was tumbling in, with deep sounds, after dark, and the revolving French light on Cape Grisnez was seen regularly bursting out and becoming obscured, as if the head of a gigantic light-keeper, in an anxious state of mind, were interposed every half-minute, to look how it was burning."

Dover, as everyone remembers, was the destination of poor little ragged David Copperfield, who, tramping wearily from London, went thither in quest of his aunt, Betsy Trotwood. In 1852 Dickens stayed for three months at No. 10, Camden Crescent, and in 1861 he took apartments at the Lord Warden Hotel.

The autumn of 1855 was spent by Dickens and his family at No. 3, Albion Villas, Folkestone, "a very pleasant little house overlooking the sea," whither he went, on the eve of the publication of "Little Dorrit," to "help his sluggish fancy." In "Reprinted Pieces" we find Folkestone disguised as "Pavilionstone," thus named after the Pavilion Hotel, originally a modest-looking building erected on the sea-front in 1843, but recently transformed into a huge establishment in order to meet the requirements of modern-day travellers *en route* to and from Boulogne. Even at the time this article was written,* the hotel is described as containing "streets of rooms" and handsome salons. Folkestone of to-day differs considerably from Folkestone of fifty years ago, having developed during the interval into a fashionable watering-place of an almost resplendent character. Nevertheless, in Dickens's presentment it is not impossible, even now, to detect the tone and colouring of old Folkestone,

* "Out of Town," first printed in *Household Words*, September 29, 1855.

with its " crooked street like a crippled ladder," etc. " Within a quarter of a century—*circa* 1830," Dickens remarks, "it was a little fishing town, and they do say that the time was when it was a little smuggling town. . . . The old little fishing and smuggling town remains. . . . There are break-neck flights of ragged steps, connecting the principal streets by backways, which will cripple the visitor in half an hour. . . . In connection with these break-neck steps I observe some wooden cottages, with tumbledown outhouses, and backyards 3 feet square, adorned with garlands of dried fish. . . . Our situation is delightful, our air delicious, and our breezy hills and downs, carpeted with wild thyme, and decorated with millions of wild flowers, are, in the faith of the pedestrian, perfect." He informs us that the harbour is a tidal one—" At low water we are a heap of mud, with an empty channel in it "—and delineates, with the sense of a keen observer, the effects of high and low tide upon the shipping, while the following is a typical example of Dickensian humour : " The very little wooden lighthouse shrinks in the idle glare of the sun. And here I may observe of the very little wooden lighthouse, that when it is lighted at night— red and green—it looks so like a medical man's, that several distracted husbands have at various times been found, on occasions of premature domestic anxiety, going round it, trying to find the night-bell !"*

Strange to relate, Maidstone, the county town, is mentioned only twice in Dickens's writings—namely, in " David Copperfield " and " The Seven Poor Travellers"; but there is a hint of his intention to

* " Out of Town."

give more prominence to it in "Edwin Drood" by making the county gaol the scene of Jasper's imprisonment. It is conjectured that Maidstone is the Muggleton of "Pickwick," there described as "a corporate town, with a mayor, burgesses, and freemen," with "an open square for the market-place, and in the centre a large inn," etc. That he knew the locality well, even at this date, there can be no doubt—indeed, it has been suggested that those remarkable Druidical stones near by, known as Kit's Coty House, with names, initials, and dates scratched thereon, may have originated the idea of Mr. Pickwick's immortal discovery of the stone inscribed by "Bill Stumps." Another Pickwickian link with the neighbourhood is Cob-tree Hall, an Elizabethan house near Aylesford, justly regarded as the original of the Manor House at Dingley Dell, which, with its surroundings, answers admirably to the description in the fourth chapter of "Pickwick."

We know that in later years he was fond of walking between Maidstone and Rochester, the seven miles constituting, in his opinion, "one of the most beautiful walks in England"; and not infrequently, when living at Gad's Hill, he would drive there with friends for a picnic, the horses bestridden by "a couple of postillions in the old red jackets of the old red royal Dover road." "It was like a holiday ride in England fifty years ago," he said to Longfellow, commenting upon one of these delightful excursions. Pilgrims in Dickens land would do well to visit Kit's Coty House and Blue Bell Hill, where, from the higher elevations, a prospect is revealed of enchanting beauty ; from such a point of vantage we behold an extensive view of the valley, in which are seen little

28

hamlets, cornfields, hop gardens, orchards, and spinneys, with the river Medway meandering in the direction of Rochester, and gradually widening as it approaches that ancient town.

The picturesque and charming city of Canterbury, as portrayed in "David Copperfield," has changed in a much less degree than many other English cathedral towns within the last twenty years or so. In that delightful story, so replete with the autobiographical element, we read: "The sunny street of Canterbury, dozing, as it were, in the hot light; . . . its old houses and gateways, and the stately gray cathedral, with the rooks sailing round the towers" (chap. xiii.). "Coming into Canterbury, I loitered through the old streets with a sober pleasure that calmed my spirits and eased my heart. . . . The venerable cathedral towers and the old jackdaws and rooks, whose airy voices made them more retired than perfect silence would have done; the battered gateways, once stuck full with statues, long thrown down, and crumbled away, like the reverential pilgrims who had gazed upon them; the still nooks, where the ivied growth of centuries crept over gabled ends and ruined walls; the ancient houses; the pastoral landscape of field, orchard, and garden—everywhere, on everything, I felt the same serener air, the same calm, thoughtful, softening spirit" (chap. xxxix.). In 1861, when giving a public Reading at Canterbury, Dickens stayed at the Fountain Hotel, in St. Margaret's Street, which is recognised locally as "the County Inn" where Mr. Dick slept when visiting David Copperfield. The "little inn" where Mr. Micawber put up is probably the Sun Hotel in Sun Street; Dr. Strong's school is the still-flourishing King's

EASTGATE HOUSE, ROCHESTER. (*Page* 217.)

The original of the Nuns' House in "Edwin Drood."

SAPSEA'S HOUSE, ROCHESTER. (*Page* 217.)

"The silent High Street of Rochester is full of gables with old beams and timbers"
("Seven Poor Travellers").

School in the cathedral precincts, its Norman staircase being an object of great antiquarian interest.

An ancient and picturesque house near the old west gate (No. 71, St. Dunstan's Street) is regarded as the probable original of Mr. Wickfield's residence; while the home of Dr. Strong is identified with the old building at the corner (No. 1) of Lady Wootton's Green.

CHAPTER X.

THE GAD'S HILL COUNTRY.

ABOUT midway between Gravesend and Rochester, on the old Dover Road, and in the parish of Higham, is Gad's Hill, immortalized both by Shakespeare and Dickens. With regard to the derivation of the name there seems to be a little doubt, some regarding it as a corruption of " God's Hill," while others incline to the belief that it must be traced to the word " gad " (*i.e.*, rogue), for, even prior to Shakespeare's time, unwary travellers were here waylaid by highwaymen, and for such audacious thefts from the person this particular spot became notorious.

In 1558 a ballad was published entitled " The Robbery at Gad's Hill," and in 1590 Sir Roger Manwood, Chief Baron of the Exchequer, wrote : " Many robberies were done in the bye-ways at Gadeshill, on the west part of Rochester and at Chatham, down on the east part of Rochester, by horse-thieves, with such fat and lusty horses as were not like hackney horses, nor far-journeying horses, and one of them sometimes wearing a vizard grey beard . . . and no man durst travel that way without great company." In the first part of Shakespeare's " King Henry the Fourth " (Act I., Scene 2) Poins thus addresses Prince Henry : " But, my lads, my lads, to-morrow morning, by four o'clock, early at Gadshill! there are pilgrims going to Canterbury with rich offerings, and traders riding to London with fat purses: I have visors for you all; you have horses for yourselves."*

To present-day pedestrians, who have no need to fear unwelcome attentions from "knights of the road," the chief attraction of this locality is the house which stands upon the brow of the hill, reposing in delightful grounds, and commanding magnificent views of the surrounding landscape. This is Gad's Hill Place, the home of Charles Dickens, where he resided from 1856 until his death on "that fateful day" in June, 1870. One of the most remarkable incidents of the novelist's life was the realization of his boyhood's ambition to live there, in the very house which he so often admired when, during his early years at Chatham, he accompanied his father on walking expeditions thence to Strood and beyond, and which, as his parent foretold, might really become his home if he worked hard, and were to be very persevering. The desire to own the property never left him; indeed, it may be said that, as time passed, his craving to possess it increased, and we may imagine his delight when, in 1855, he learned from his trusty henchman, W. H. Wills, that the place was available for purchase.

Having spent the final years of his active career at Gad's Hill Place, it is natural that Gad's Hill Place and its environment should be regarded as the very heart of Dickens land, so replete is it with Dickensian memories and associations.

* In the same play, curiously enough, one of the minor characters is named "Gadshill."

Gad's Hill Place is a red brick building, with bay windows and a porch in the principal front, a slated roof with dormers, surmounted by a cupola or bell-turret, the latter a conspicuous and familiar object to all accustomed to travel by road between Gravesend and Rochester. The house was erected in 1779 by a then well-known character in those parts, one Thomas Stevens, an illiterate man who had been an hostler, and who, after marrying his employer's widow, adopted the brewing business, amassed wealth, and eventually became Mayor of Rochester. On relinquishing the business he retired to his country seat at Gad's Hill, and at his death the house was purchased by the Rev. James Lynn (father of the late Mrs. Lynn Linton, the authoress), who, like Dickens, had fallen in love with the house when a youth, and resolved to buy it as soon as the opportunity offered. It was not until 1831 that he was enabled to take up his residence there, and Mrs. Lynn Linton, in recording her impressions of her home at that date, recalled the liveliness of the road : " Between seventy and eighty coaches, 'vans,' and mail-carts passed our house during the day, besides private carriages, specially those of travellers posting to or from Dover. Regiments, too, often passed on their way to Gravesend, where they embarked for India ; and ships' companies, paid off, rowdy, and half-tipsy, made the road really dangerous for the time being. We used to lock the two gates when we heard them coming, shouting and singing, up the hill, and we had to stand many a mimic siege from the bluejackets trying to force their way in."* To

* "A Week's Tramp in Dickens Land," by W. R. Hughes, 1891.

RESTORATION HOUSE, ROCHESTER. (*Page* 217.)

The "Satis House" of "Great Expectations." Charles II. slept here on the eve of the Restoration, May, 1660.

counteract these obvious drawbacks there were natural advantages — the luxuriant gardens, orchard, and shrubberies, while the trees near the house offered a veritable sanctuary for song-birds. The worthy clergyman occupied Gad's Hill Place until his decease in 1855, when, for want of an heir, the property had to be sold. Shortly afterwards his daughter and W. H. Wills met at a dinner-party, and in the course of conversation it transpired that the estate would presently be in the market. On learning this, Dickens immediately entered into negotiations for acquiring it, with the result that before many months had elapsed he became the owner. " I have always in passing looked to see if it was to be sold or let," he wrote to his friend M. de Cerjat, "and it has never been to me like any other house, and it has never changed at all."

After drawing a cheque (on March 14, 1856) for the amount of the purchase-money, £1,790, he discovered that, by an extraordinary coincidence, it was a Friday, the day of the week on which (as he frequently remarked) all the important events of his life had happened, so that he and his family had come to regard that day of the week as his lucky day.

Dickens did not, however, obtain possession of the coveted house until February of the following year, after which, for a brief period, he made it merely a summer abode, Tavistock House being his town residence during the rest of the year. In April, 1857, he stayed with his wife and sister-in-law at Waite's Hotel, Gravesend, to be at hand to superintend the beginning of a scheme of alterations and improvements in his new home, which were carried on for the space of several months. The winter of

1859-1860 was the last spent at Tavistock House, and he and his family then settled down at Gad's Hill. "I am on my little Kentish freehold," he observed to M. de Cerjat, "looking on as pretty a view out of my study window as you will find in a long day's English ride. My little place is a grave red-brick house, which I have added to and stuck bits upon in all manner of ways, so that it is as pleasantly irregular, and as violently opposed to all architectural ideas, as the most hopeful man could possibly desire. The robbery was committed before the door, on the man with the treasure, and Falstaff ran away from the identical spot of ground now covered by the room in which I write. A little rustic alehouse, called the Sir John Falstaff, is over the way, has been over the way ever since, in honour of the event. Cobham Woods and Park are behind the house, the distant Thames in front, the Medway, with Rochester and its old castle and cathedral, on one side. The whole stupendous property is on the old Dover Road."

Continued ownership brought increased liking, and he was never tired of devising and superintending improvements, such as the addition of a new drawing-room and conservatory, the construction of a well (a process "like putting Oxford Street endwise"), and the engineering of a tunnel under the road, connecting the front-garden with the shrubbery, with its noble cedars, where, in the midst of foliage, was erected the Swiss châlet presented to him in 1865 by Fechter, the actor, and which now stands in Cobham Park. Concerning this châlet—in an upper compartment of which he was fond of working, remote from disturbing sounds—he sent a charming account of his environment to his American friend

THE BULL HOTEL, ROCHESTER. (*Page* 219.)

"*Good house—nice beds*" ("*Pickwick*")

James T. Fields: "Divers birds sing here all day, and the nightingales all night. The place is lovely and in perfect order. . . . I have put five mirrors in the châlet where I write, and they reflect and refract, in all kinds of ways, the leaves that are quivering at the windows, and the great fields of waving corn, and the sail-dotted river. My room is up among the branches of the trees, and the birds and the butterflies fly in and out, and the green branches shoot in at the open windows, and the lights and shadows of the clouds come and go with the rest of the company. The scent of the flowers, and, indeed, of everything that is growing for miles and miles, is most delicious."

Externally, the main building of Gad's Hill Place underwent but little alteration, presenting throughout the period of the owner's occupation much the same appearance as when he knew it in the days of his childhood, the back of the building becoming gradually hidden from view by clustering masses of ivy and Virginia creeper. One of the bedrooms was transformed into a study, which he lined with books and occasionally wrote in; but the study proper (called by him the library) was the front room on the ground-floor, on the right of the entrance-hall, rendered familiar by the large engraving published in the *Graphic* at the time of the novelist's death. With regard to this study, or library, it may be mentioned that it was his delight to be surrounded by a variety of objects for his eye to rest upon in the intervals of actual writing, prominent among them being a bronze group representing a couple of frogs in the act of fighting a duel with swords, and a statuette of a French dog-fancier, with his living stock-in-trade tucked under his arms and in his pockets, while a vase of flowers invariably graced his writing-table. A noteworthy feature of his sanctum was the door, the inner side of which he disguised by means of imitation book-backs, transferred thither from Tavistock House ; these are still preserved as a " fixture." These book-backs, with their humorous titles, create considerable interest and amusement for such as are privileged to enter the apartment so intimately associated with " Boz."

Among those invited to his attractive " Kentish freehold," as Dickens frequently termed it, "where cigars and lemons grew on all the trees," was Sir Joseph Paxton, the famous landscape gardener and designer of the Crystal Palace. Hans Andersen, another honoured guest, received most agreeable impressions of Gad's Hill Place. He described the breakfast-room as "a model of comfort and holiday brightness. The windows were overhung, outside, with a profusion of blooming roses, and one looked out over the garden to green fields and the hills beyond Rochester." Dickens's happiest hours in his Gad's Hill home were those when it was filled with cherished friends, both English and American, to whom he played the part of an ideal host, devoting the greater portion of each day to their comfort and amusement, and accompanying them on pedestrian excursions to Rochester and other favourite localities in the neighbourhood, or driving with them to more remote places, such as Maidstone and Canterbury. But what seemed to afford him the utmost delight were the walks with friends to the charming village of Cobham, there to refresh at the famous Leather Bottle, the quaint roadside alehouse where, as every reader of " Pickwick " remembers, the disconsolate

Mr. Tupman was discovered at the parlour table having just enjoyed a hearty meal of "roast fowl, bacon, ale, and etceteras, and looking as unlike a man who had taken his leave of the world as possible." The Pickwickian traditions of this popular house of refreshment are maintained by the enthusiastic landlord, who realizes the importance of preserving the Dickensian associations. The room in which Mr. Tupman drowned his sorrows in the comfort afforded by a substantial meal remains practically the same to-day, with this difference, that the walls are covered with portraits, engravings, autograph letters, and other interesting items relating to the novelist and his writings—a veritable Dickens museum. Cobham Hall, the Elizabethan mansion of Lord Darnley, with its magnificent park, where the Fechter châlet was re-erected after Dickens's death, and especially Cobham Woods, always proved irresistible attractions to the "Master," and he and his dogs enjoying their constitutional were a familiar sight to his neighbours.

The villages of Shorne and Chalk, with their ancient churches and peaceful churchyards, he frequently visited with "a strange recurring fondness." Mr. E. Laman Blanchard has recorded that he often met, and exchanged salutations with, Dickens during his pedestrian excursions on the highroad leading from Rochester to Gravesend, and generally they passed each other at about the same spot—at the outskirts of the village of Chalk, where a picturesque lane branched off towards Shorne and Cobham. "Here," says Mr. Blanchard, "the brisk walk of Charles Dickens was always slackened, and he never failed to glance meditatively for a few moments at the windows of a corner house on the southern side of the road, advantageously situated for commanding views of the river and the far-stretching landscape beyond. It was in that house he lived immediately after his marriage, and there many of the earlier chapters of 'Pickwick' were written."

The village of Cooling, standing so bleak and solitary in the Kentish fenland bordering the southern banks of the Thames, possessed a weird fascination for "Boz." Here, in the midst of those dreary marshes, much of the local colouring of "Great Expectations" was obtained. Indeed, the story opens with the night scene between Pip and the escaped convict in Cooling churchyard, and in the same chapter we have Pip's early impressions of the strange and desolate neighbourhood in which he lived with Mr. and Mrs. Joe Gargery. "Ours was the marsh country, down by the river, within, as the river wound, twenty miles from the sea. My first most vivid and broad impression of the identity of things seems to me to have been gained on a memorable raw afternoon towards evening. At such a time I found out for certain that this bleak place overgrown with nettles was the churchyard, and that Philip Pirrip, late of this parish, and also Georgina, wife of the above, were dead and buried; and that Alexander, Bartholomew, Abraham, Tobias, and Roger, infant children of the aforesaid, were also dead and buried; and that the dark, flat wilderness beyond the churchyard, intersected with dykes, and mounds, and gates, with scattered cattle feeding on it, was the marshes; and that the low leaden line beyond was the river; and that the distant savage lair, from which the wind was rushing, was the sea; and that the small bundle of shivers growing afraid of it all, and beginning to cry, was Pip."

" The marshes," Pip continues, " were just a long black horizontal line then, . . . and the river was just another horizontal line, not nearly so broad nor yet so black ; and the sky was just a row of long angry red lines and dense black lines intermixed. On the edge of the river I could faintly make out the only two black things in all the prospect that seemed to be standing upright. One of these was the beacon by which the sailors steered—like an unhooped cask upon a pole—an ugly thing when you were near it ; the other, a gibbet, with some chains hanging to it which had once held a pirate." Then, in a later chapter, he refers to the old battery out on the marshes. " It was pleasant and quiet out there," he says, "with the sails on the river passing beyond the earthwork, and sometimes, when the tide was low, looking as if they belonged to sunken ships that were still sailing on at the bottom of the water."

Visitors to Cooling cannot fail to notice in the churchyard a long row of curious gravestones which mark the resting-place of members of the Comport family of Cowling Court (Cooling was originally called Cowling), these memorials dating from 1771, the year recorded on a large headstone standing in close proximity. These suggested to Dickens, of course, the idea of the " five little stone lozenges " under which the five little brothers of Pip lay buried. Within a short distance from the churchyard we may identify, in a short row of cottages, the original of Joe's forge, while an old-fashioned inn with a weather-board exterior, and bearing the sign of the

Horseshoe and Castle, is regarded as the prototype
of the Three Jolly Bargemen, a favourite resort of
Joe Gargery after his day's work at the forge.

The ancient and picturesque city of Rochester, so
beloved by Dickens and so replete with memories of
the "Master," deserves a chapter to itself. With
the exception of London, no town figures so frequently
or so prominently in his books as Rochester, from
"The Pickwick Papers" to the unfinished romance
of "The Mystery of Edwin Drood," where it is
thinly disguised as "Cloisterham." Dickens's acquaintance with Rochester began in the days of his boyhood, when he lived with his father at Chatham,
and, as a natural result of his unusual powers of
observation, he even then stored up his youthful
impressions of the quaint old houses, the Cathedral,
and its neighbour, the rugged ruins of the Norman
Castle overlooking the Medway. How those juvenile
impressions received something of a shock in after-
years we are informed by Forster, for childhood
exaggerates what it sees, and Rochester High Street
he remembered as a thoroughfare at least as wide as
Regent Street, whereas it proved to his maturer
judgment to be "little better than a lane," while the
public clock in it, once supposed by him to be the
finest clock in the world, proved eventually to be
"as moon-faced and weak a clock as a man's eyes
ever saw." Even the grave-looking Town Hall,
"which had appeared to him once so glorious
a structure" that he associated it in his mind
with Aladdin's palace, he reluctantly realized as
being, in reality, nothing more than "a mere
mean little heap of bricks, like a chapel gone
demented." "Ah! who was I," he observes on

reflection, " that I should quarrel with the town for being changed to me, when I myself had come back, so changed, to it? All my early readings and early imaginations dated from this place, and I took them away so full of innocent construction and guileless belief, and I brought them back so worn and torn, so much the wiser and so much the worse !"

Rochester has undergone many topographical changes (not necessarily for the better) since that memorable morning in 1827 when Mr. Pickwick leaned over the balustrades of the old stone bridge "contemplating nature and waiting for breakfast." To begin with, the bridge itself has been demolished, and an elliptical iron structure takes its place. The view, too, which Mr. Pickwick admired of the banks of the Medway, with the cornfields, pastures, and windmills, is more obscured to-day by that discomforting symbol of commercialism, smoke, so constantly pouring from the ever-increasing number of lofty shafts appertaining to the various cement works which flourish here. From the other side of the bridge Mr. Pickwick could obtain a pleasant glimpse of the river, with its numerous sailing-barges, in the direction of Chatham ; but the prospect, alas! is now completely blotted out by hideous railway viaducts. Happily, in spite of modern innovations, those who appreciate the old-world air of our English cities will find much to charm them in the precincts of the Cathedral, sufficiently remote from the bustle and noise of the High Street to enable it to preserve the quiet serenity which invariably encompasses our venerable minsters. Besides the picturesque stone gateways here, much remains in the High Street and elsewhere to remind us of what Rochester looked like in days of old ; as Dickens writes in " The Seven Poor Travellers ": " The silent High Street of Rochester is full of gables, with old beams and timbers carved into strange faces." Of these surviving specimens of ancient domestic architecture, many will regard Eastgate House as the most interesting from an archæological point of view, while to the Dickens student there is an additional attraction in the fact that it is the original of the Nuns' House in "Edwin Drood," the boarding-school for young ladies over which Miss Twinkleton presided, and where Rosa Bud received her education.

For many years during the last century East-gate House was actually in use as a ladies' school, and eventually became the headquarters of the Rochester Men's Institute. Quite recently the civic authorities, with commendable good sense, availed themselves of the opportunity of acquiring the property, which they have thoroughly and tastefully reinstated and converted into a public museum ; and I must add to this statement the significant fact that a room has been permanently set apart for an exhibition of mementoes of Charles Dickens—both gifts and loans—thus, in a sense, stultifying the old proverb, that "a prophet is not without honour save in his own country." On one of the inside beams of Eastgate House is carved the date " 1591," and the rooms are adorned with carved mantelpieces and plaster enrichments.

Nearly opposite Eastgate House is another picturesque half-timbered building, which, with its three gables and its projecting bay - windows supported by carved brackets, is a veritable

CHARLES DICKENS IN 1868.

From a Photograph by Mason.   Reproduced by kind permission of Messrs. Chapman and Hall.

ornament to this portion of the High Street. We recognise it as the one-time residence of two of Dickens's characters, viz., of Mr. Sapsea, the auctioneer in "Edwin Drood"—"Mr. Sapsea's premises are in the High Street over against the Nuns' House"—and of Mr. Pumblechook, the seed merchant in "Great Expectations." But there exists in Rochester a specimen of domestic architecture of even greater interest than those just described. This is Restoration House, pleasantly situated facing an open space called "The Vines"—the Monks' Vineyard of "Edwin Drood." Restoration House is the Satis House of "Great Expectations," where lived that strange creature Miss Havisham; as a matter of fact, there exists in Rochester an actual Satis House, the name being transferred by Dickens to the old manor-house associated with Pip and Estella, and with that "immensely rich and grim lady" the aforesaid Miss Havisham. Restoration House, which dates from Elizabeth's reign, afforded temporary lodging to Charles II. in 1660, who subsequently honoured his host, Sir Francis Clarke, with a series of large tapestries of English workmanship, which are still preserved.

In Rochester High Street the visitor cannot fail to observe, on the north side, a stone-fronted building with three gables, having over the entrance-gate a curiously inscribed tablet, which reads thus:

RICHARD WATTS, ESQUIRE,
by his Will dated 22nd August, 1579,
founded this Charity
for Six Poor Travellers,
who, not being Rogues or Proctors,
May receive gratis for one Night
Lodging, Entertainment,
and Fourpence each.

30

This quaint institution, founded by Master Richard Watts, Rochester's sixteenth-century philanthropist, still flourishes, and it is an exceptional thing for a night to pass without its full complement of applicants for temporary board and lodging, according to the terms formulated by the charitable founder, by whom also were established several almshouses situated on the Maidstone Road, endowed for the support and maintenance of impoverished Rochester townsfolk. Watts's Charity, in the High Street, is immortalized by Dickens in the Christmas number of *Household Words*, 1854, entitled " The Seven Poor Travellers," in which the story of Richard Doubledick is one of the most touching things the novelist ever penned. Dickens, doubtless, frequently visited the Charity during his Gad's Hill days, for he delighted in escorting his American friends and others around the old city, and pointing out to them its more striking features. In one of the visitors' books, in which many distinguished names are recorded, will be found (under date May 11, 1854, the year of publication of the above-mentioned Christmas number) the bold autographs of Charles Dickens and his friend Mark Lemon.

An account of Dickensian Rochester which omitted to mention the Bull Inn would be unpardonably incomplete. The Bull, the historic Bull of " The Pickwick Papers," which the imperturbable Mr. Jingle averred to Mr. Pickwick was a " good house " with " nice beds," is naturally one of the principal sights of Rochester from the point of view of the Dickens admirer and student, and Dickens pilgrims from all parts of the world immediately direct their steps thither on their arrival in the city. Situated on the south side of the High Street, within a short distance of Rochester Bridge, the Bull and Victoria Hotel (to give its full designation) has an exceedingly unprepossessing brick frontage, its only decorative feature being the Royal Arms over the entrance. Why does the famous coaching-inn bear the double sign of the Bull and *Victoria?* It originated in this way: One stormy day at the end of November, 1836, the late Queen Victoria (then Princess), with her mother the Duchess of Kent, stopped at the Bull; they were travelling to London from Dover, and the royal party, warned of the possibility of their carriage being upset in crossing the bridge, stayed at the hostelry all night, the apartment in which England's future Sovereign slept being the identical room previously allocated to Mr. Tupman in "Pickwick." Naturally, in order to commemorate the royal visit, the inn was called by its present designation, although popularly known simply as the Bull. Some portions of the establishment still retain their old-world characteristics, although it must be confessed that the appearance of the majority of the dormitories and living-rooms partakes more of the early Victorian period than of an earlier date; one might conjecture, too, that the house had been refronted during the beginning of the nineteenth century. The place is replete with Pickwickian associations; here we may see the veritable staircase where the stormy interview occurred between the irate Dr. Slammer and Alfred Jingle; here, too, is the actual ball-room, which, with its glass chandeliers and "elevated den" for the musicians, has remained unaltered since the description of it appeared in " Pickwick." The sleeping apartments of Messrs. Tupman and Winkle ("Winkle's bedroom is inside mine," said Mr. Tupman) may be identified in those numbered 13 and 19 respectively, while Mr. Pickwick's room is distinguished as "No. 17," which tradition declares was occupied on at least one occasion by Dickens himself, and now contains some pieces of furniture formerly in use at Gad's Hill Place. Although much less prominently than in " Pickwick," the Bull is introduced in other works of Dickens. It appears, for example, in one of the " Sketches by Boz," entitled " The great Winglebury Duel" (written before " Pickwick"), where " the little town of Great Winglebury " and "the Winglebury Arms " are undoubtedly intended for Rochester and its principal hostelry. In "Great Expectations " the Bull is again introduced as the Blue Boar, where it will be remembered that, in honour of the important event of Pip being bound apprentice to Joe Gargery (the premium having been paid by Miss Havisham), arrangements were made for a dinner at the Blue Boar, attended by the servile Pumblechook, the Hubbles, and Mr. Wopsle. "Among the festivities indulged in rather late in the evening," observes Pip, who did not particularly enjoy himself on the occasion, " Mr. Wopsle gave us Collins's Ode, and 'threw his blood-stain'd sword in thunder down,' with such effect that a waiter came in and said, 'The commercials underneath sent up their compliments, and it wasn't the Tumblers' Arms!'"

It was recently rumoured that the Bull, not proving satisfactorily remunerative, stood in danger of demolition, and that a new hotel, possessing those improvements which present-day travellers regard as indispensable, would be erected on the site. Needless to say, all Dickens lovers would deplore the realization of such a proposal.

*   *   *   *   *

I venture to conclude with a few supplementary remarks concerning Gad's Hill Place, the bourne to which all devout Dickens worshippers make a pilgrimage, among whom our American cousins are undoubtedly the most ardent enthusiasts.

Dickens paid the purchase-money for Gad's Hill Place on March 14, 1856; it was a Friday, and handing the cheque for £1,790 to Wills, he observed: "Now, isn't it an extraordinary thing—look at the day—Friday! I have been nearly drawing it half a dozen times, when the lawyers have not been ready, and here it comes round upon a Friday as a matter of course." He frequently remarked that all the important events of his life happened to him on a Friday. Referring to this transaction, Mrs. Lynn Linton, in "My Literary Life," says: "We sold it cheap, £1,700, and we asked £40 for the ornamental timber. To this Dickens and his agent made an objection; so we had an arbitrator, who awarded us £70, which was in the nature of a triumph." The house contains fourteen rooms and the usual offices; there are greenhouses, stables, a kitchen-garden, a farmyard, etc., the property comprising eleven acres of land, a considerable portion of which Dickens subsequently acquired through private negotiations with the respective owners.

At Gad's Hill Dickens produced some of his best work. During the period of his residence here

(1857-1870), he wrote the concluding chapters of "Little Dorrit," "A Tale of Two Cities," "Great Expectations," "Our Mutual Friend," and the fragment of "The Mystery of Edwin Drood," concerning which Longfellow entertained a very high opinion, believing that it promised to be one of the finest of his stories ; he also contributed to *All The Year Round* those remarkable papers published under the general title of " The Uncommercial Traveller," perhaps the most delightful of his minor writings.

It was on June 8, 1870, that Dickens, while at dinner, suddenly became very ill and almost immediately lost consciousness, from which he never recovered. On the following day his spirit fled, and it is no exaggeration to say that never has the death of a distinguished man caused greater consternation throughout the civilized world than did the unexpected passing of the great novelist.

Not many weeks had elapsed after this sad event when Gad's Hill Place and its contents were disposed of by public auction. The house, with eight acres of meadow-land, was virtually bought in by Charles Dickens the younger at the much enhanced price of £7,500. For a time the novelist's eldest son made it his home ; but, as he informed the present writer, the increasing needs of his large and growing young family could not be sufficiently accommodated, and this determined him to sell the place—a decision which naturally caused those interested in its fate to fear the possibility of its falling into the hands of an unsympathetic proprietor, who would fail to appreciate or to cherish the unique associations. After being a considerable time on the market, the property was purchased in 1879 by Captain (now Major) Austin F.

Budden, then of the 12th Kent Artillery Volunteers, and Mayor of Rochester from that year until 1881.

It was during Major Budden's occupancy of Gad's Hill Place, in the late summer of 1888, that I accompanied my friend the late Mr. W. R. Hughes (author of "A Week's Tramp in Dickens Land") on a memorable visit to this famous residence. We met with a most friendly reception from the genial host and his wife, and were privileged to inspect every point of interest within and without—the library with its curious dummy book-backs, the dining-room where "the Master" succumbed to the fatal seizure, the conservatory (his "last improvement") the well (with the Major's mare, Tell-tale, busily drawing water), the grave of the pet canary, the tunnel under the Dover road, etc. Perhaps the most unexpected treat was the view from the roof of the building, whence it is easy to realize the charming environment. Looking northward from this high elevation, we may view the marshes, which flat and dreary expanse is relieved by a glimpse of the Thames, widening as it approaches seaward, and bearing upon its silvery bosom a number of vessels, both steamships and sailing ships, the ruddy brown sails of the barges giving colour to the scene. To the east is the valley of the Medway, the prospect including a distant view of Rochester, crowned by the rugged keep of the old Castle and by the Cathedral tower.* To the south the beautifully undulating

---

* It is generally admitted that the tower of Rochester Cathedral is altogether out of harmony with the rest of this Norman edifice. It was designed by Cottingham, and erected in 1825 to replace the earlier tower, which was surmounted by a thick stunted spire. A fund has been raised to which

greensward of Cobham Park and the umbrageous Cobham Woods complete this wonderful panorama of Nature.

In 1889 (the year following that of our visit) Gad's Hill Place narrowly escaped destruction by fire. It is the old story—a leakage of gas, a naked light, and an explosion; happily, Major Budden's supply of hand-grenades did their duty and saved the building. Shortly afterwards the house and accompanying land were again in the market, and in 1890 a purchaser was found in the Hon. Francis Law Latham, Advocate-General at Bombay. This gentleman, however, could not enter into possession until his return to England a few months later. Meanwhile Major Budden took up his residence elsewhere, so that during a part of the year 1891 Gad's Hill Place was empty and deserted, pathetically contrasting with those ever-to-be-remembered days when Charles Dickens and his hosts of friends enlivened the neighbourhood with cricket matches, athletic sports, etc. Mr. Latham is still the tenant-owner of Gad's Hill Place, and, needless to say, thoroughly appreciates the unique associations of his attractive home, where he hopes to spend in quiet and secluded retirement the remaining years of a busy life.

---

the late Dean, Dr. Reynolds Hole, so generously contributed, for the purpose of substituting a tower approximating in character the older structure.

At the time of publication (December, 1904) the lowering and re-casing of the tower and the addition of a 66 ft. spire are completed.

INDEX

The titles of the writings of Dickens are printed in italics.

BILLING AND SONS, LTD., PRINTERS, GUILDFORD

THE
THACKERAY COUNTRY

By LEWIS MELVILLE

Large Crown 8vo. 3/6 Cloth

Containing 32 full-page Illustrations and a Map

"THE THACKERAY COUNTRY" treats of those localities which are of primary interest to those who are acquainted with the life and writings of the great novelist. Mr. Melville deals with Thackeray's London homes and the salient features and associations of their neighbourhood. He goes with Thackeray to Paris, and follows the course of his travels on the Continent and in America, giving special attention to those places that are made the background of well-known scenes in the novels. He is careful to give all the biographical information connected with Thackeray's residences from his arrival in England from India at the age of six until his death.

The volume is illustrated with thirty-two full-page plates reproduced from photographs specially taken for the book by Catharine W. Barnes Ward, and a map.

CONTENTS

PUBLISHED BY
ADAM AND CHARLES BLACK . SOHO SQUARE . LONDON, W.

1

THE
FASCINATION OF LONDON

EDITED BY SIR WALTER BESANT

Foolscap 8vo.   Price **1/6** net each, Cloth

Bound in Limp Leather, price 2/- net each

Each Volume contains a Map of the district and a Frontispiece

VOLUMES READY

SOME PRESS OPINIONS

"We have here, in fact, just what will give people who do not know their London a new interest in every walk they take, and indicate to those who want more the lines on which their studies may be conducted."—*Times*.

"It is scarcely necessary to write any words of commendation when the great knowledge of the editor and the literary charm with which he always writes of London are taken into consideration."—*Pall Mall Gazette*.

"The book, and the series of which it is a part, will be welcomed by those who already possess that detailed knowledge of London and its associations in which Sir Walter Besant delighted, and a perusal of its pages by those less fortunate will do much to add to the number of his disciples."—*County Council Times*.

PUBLISHED BY

ADAM AND CHARLES BLACK . SOHO SQUARE . LONDON, **W.**

THE
ROMANCE OF LONDON

By GORDON HOME

Containing 12 full-page Illustrations in Colour and 6 Line Drawings in the text. Fcap. 4to., Cloth

Price **1/6** net

(By post, price 1/9)

PUBLISHERS' NOTE

THE ROMANCE OF LONDON, as the title is intended to convey, is a book designed to bring before the reader pictorially, and with interestingly written descriptive matter, the survivals of the London of the Middle Ages, of Tudor times, and of the picturesque seventeenth century.

That these relics are so numerous will surprise many people who have not cared to explore London's antiquities. How many, for instance, have seen all the Norman buildings in the City? The Keep of the Tower, with its perfectly-preserved Chapel, is the chief of the Norman structures ; but besides this there is the grand old Church of St. Bartholomew-the-Great, West Smithfield, the crypt of St. Mary-le-Bow Church in Cheapside, and the newly-discovered Norman portions of the crypt beneath the Guildhall.

The magnificent Norman nave of St. Paul's which survived the Great Fire of 1666, was unfortunately demolished when the scheme of restoration was abandoned.

The 12 illustrations in colour include Westminster Abbey, The Tower, St. Paul's, The Temple, Lincoln's Inn, Cloth Fair, and the Pool of London, and amongst those in black and white are Charterhouse, the old houses in Holborn, details of Westminster Abbey and the Tower, and St. John's Gateway, Clerkenwell.

PUBLISHED BY

ADAM AND CHARLES BLACK . SOHO SQUARE . LONDON, W.

3